How the
INTERNET
CHANGED HISTORY

How the INTERNET CHANGED HISTORY

by Carol Hand

CONTENT CONSULTANT

Janet Abbate, PhD

Associate Professor, Science & Technology in Society

Virginia Tech

ESSENTIAL LIBRARY OF INVENTIONS

Essential Library

An Imprint of Abdo Publishing | abdopublishing.com

abdopublishing.com

Published by Abdo Publishing, a division of ABDO, PO Box 398166, Minneapolis, Minnesota 55439. Copyright © 2016 by Abdo Consulting Group, Inc. International copyrights reserved in all countries. No part of this book may be reproduced in any form without written permission from the publisher. Essential Library™ is a trademark and logo of Abdo Publishing.

Printed in the United States of America, North Mankato, Minnesota
052015
092015

Cover Photos: Shutterstock Images (left), Iñaki Antoñana Plaza/iStockphoto (right)
Interior Photos: Shutterstock Images, 10, 26–27, 35, 40–41 (foreground), 40–41 (background), 86–87, 99 (top); Iñaki Antoñana Plaza/iStockphoto, 15; Marcio Jose Sanchez/AP Images, 2, 96; Damian Dovarganes/AP Images, 6–7; iStockphoto, 13, 36 (left), 36 (right), 71, 99 (bottom); AP Images, 16–17, 20, 28, 74–75; Apic/Getty Images, 24 (left); Brian Cahn/ZumaPress/Corbis, 24 (right); Ed Quinn/Corbis, 31; Justin Sullivan/Getty Images News/Thinkstock, 38, 49; Elise Amendola/AP Images, 42–43; Al Grillo/AP Images, 47; Gautam Singh/AP Images, 50–51; Jerome Brunet/ZumaPress/Newscom, 53; Rob Wilson/iStockphoto, 57; Nadine Rupp/Getty Images News/Thinkstock, 59; Jen Grantham/iStockphoto, 61; Gil C./Shutterstock Images, 62–63; Martia Punts/iStockphoto, 67; Spencer Platt/Getty Images News/Thinkstock, 78; Bernhard Classen/ZumaPress/Newscom, 81; Charles Dharapak/AP Images, 83; Richard Vogel/AP Images, 91; Kevin Wolf/Avaaz/AP Images, 94; Ann Hermes/The Christian Science Monitor/AP Images, 98 (right); Dan Carter/The Daily Journal of Commerce/AP Images, 98 (left)

Editor: Mirella Miller
Series Designer: Craig Hinton

Library of Congress Control Number: 2015930959

Cataloging-in-Publication Data

Hand, Carol.
   How the internet changed history / Carol Hand.
      p. cm. -- (Essential library of inventions)
Includes bibliographical references and index.
ISBN 978-1-62403-783-2
1. Internet--History--Juvenile literature.   2. Inventions--Juvenile literature.
I. Title.
004.67--dc23

                                            2015930959

CONTENTS

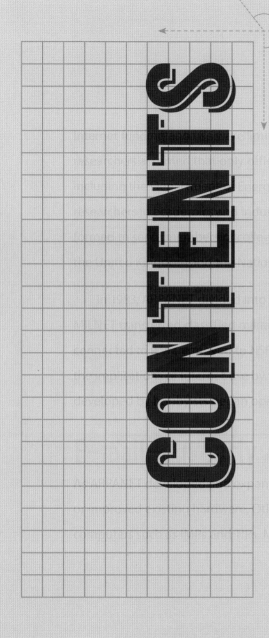

CHAPTER 1

THE INTERNET IS BORN

T he date was October 29, 1969. At 10:30 p.m., Dr. Leonard Kleinrock, a professor at the University of California, Los Angeles (UCLA), stood in his laboratory, surrounded by fellow professors and students. He connected a computer to a large metal box the size and shape of a refrigerator. The box was an interface message processor (IMP). At the same time, several hundred miles away at Stanford Research Institute in California, a second computer was connected to another IMP. Long-distance telephone circuits connected the two IMPs to each other.

In 2007, Dr. Kleinrock reenacted how the first Internet communication was made between the Stanford Research Institute and UCLA.

THE INTERFACE MESSAGE PROCESSOR

Physicist and computer designer Wesley Clark first proposed the interface message processor (IMP). IMPs would be minicomputers designed to handle the connection of computers to Advanced Research Projects Agency Network (ARPANET). They would provide an interface between their home computer and distant computers. All IMPs would use a single consistent software program, rather than needing a separate program to connect each computer. In December 1968, the Defense Department's Advanced Research Projects Agency (ARPA) awarded the contract to design the IMP to Bolt Baranek and Newman, based in Cambridge, Massachusetts.

Seated at the UCLA computer was Charley Kline, an undergraduate student. Kline's job was to type the first message to be sent over the brand-new Internet—the command *LOGIN*. First, Kline got on the telephone with his counterpart at Stanford. Then, he typed the letter *L*. Over the phone, Kline asked, "Have you got the *L*?" The Stanford colleague replied, "Got the *L*." Then Kline typed the *O*. "Have you got the *O*?" "Got the *O*."[1] Then he typed the G, and the Stanford system crashed. By accident, the first message sent over the Internet was *LO*. On the next attempt, the word *LOGIN* arrived safely. Kleinrock later described this event as "the day the infant Internet uttered its first words."[2] Of course, at that point the Internet was so new, it did not yet have a name.

Many exciting things happened in 1969, but to most people, the event that surpassed all others was the July 20 Apollo 11 moon landing. At the time, most technology buffs thought this would be the decade's supreme moment—the moment that would define the future. But it was the event almost no one noticed, when two computers several hundred miles apart first talked to each other that would more profoundly change the way humans live.

Life before the Internet

Consider a teen living in 1969. It is Monday morning and she has not talked with her best friend since Friday. Last night, her boyfriend called and they talked for five minutes before her mother made her hang up. The phone is on the wall in the hallway, near the living room where the family is often watching television. She has little privacy. She really wants to talk with her friend about her phone conversation. Would her boyfriend ask her to the prom? Would her mother take her shopping to buy a new dress? Plus, she is worried about her term paper. She has to go to the public library to do research—if any books are available. How wonderful, she thought, if she could talk with her friends privately anytime she wanted, do her research, and maybe even buy her dress, without all this hassle.

LEONARD KLEINROCK

Dr. Leonard Kleinrock received his PhD from Massachusetts Institute of Technology (MIT) in 1963. He has spent the last 50 years at UCLA as a distinguished professor of computer science. Kleinrock has received many honors for his leadership in founding the Internet. In 2007, he received the National Medal of Science, the highest science honor in the United States. Dr. Kleinrock is now working on "smart spaces," whereby, he says, "cyberspace comes out from behind the screen . . . and moves out into your physical space so that there will be intelligence and embedded technology in the walls of your room, in your desk, in your fingernails."[3]

Teenagers can do homework and research on tablet computers they carry in their backpacks.

Thanks to the Internet, teenagers in the year 2015 and beyond are constantly connected not only to friends and family, but also to people and information worldwide. They can store much of their lives "in the cloud" to be retrieved by anyone at any time. They can take a photo and send it to friends, order a pizza, download music and movies, find a location, check the weather, or watch a football game—all with pocket-sized smartphones. But many technological advances occurred between those first steps in the 1960s and the Internet of today.

TRACING THE INTERNET

Technology writer Andrew Blum started with only a vague notion of the Internet. "To be online was to be disembodied, reduced to eyes and fingertips," he said. "There was the virtual world and the physical world, cyberspace and real places, and never the two shall meet."[5] Blum's view of the Internet changed radically when his own portion of it failed. The technician sent to solve the problem tested electronic cables and switches, and eventually he traced the problem outdoors——to a squirrel chewing through the rubber coating on a wire, which in turn was attached to a metal box on a pole. Suddenly, Blum realized the Internet did not exist in a cloud. It consisted of physical structures——cords, wires, and boxes—— all of which led somewhere.

The Internet is a vast electronic communication network that connects many smaller networks around the world. In other words, it is a global network connecting millions of computers in more than 100 countries.[4] But what exactly does the Internet consist of? It is vastly more complex than its creators could have imagined. People use it constantly, but few stop to consider its components. A teenager gets onto the Internet, accesses a browser, and pulls up his or her Instagram. Where did the page come from? How did it get from its source to the computer? Where is it stored when no one is using it? A girl sends a text to her mother who is on a business trip on the other side of the country. How does the text travel from her cell phone to her mother's? Out of millions of cell phones in that distant city, how does the text pinpoint only her mother's phone?

How the Internet Sends Messages

The purpose of the Internet is to send messages—billions and billions of them. Some are simple text messages. Others are encyclopedic amounts of information on every topic imaginable. Some are photographs, videos, or movies. Others are maps, blueprints, financial information, or military codes. All of this information must be broken down into digital code—codes composed of ones and zeroes. This digital information travels from the building where it originates, through a series of tubes buried along roads and railroad tracks, across the bottom of the ocean, and on to other buildings around the world. Its travel is anything but random. Each tiny packet of information is labeled with its own unique address and its destination's unique address. The information is sent from a single router—today's equivalent of an IMP—to nearby routers, which then transfer it to routers near them. In this way, the unique packet of information reaches around the world. Billions of information packets zip past continually, each one uniquely labeled to be decoded at its destination.

Physically, the tubes contain fiber-optic cables, bundles of glass strands each as thin as a human hair. These cables carry digital information, in the form of light, across very long distances. Computers at the beginning and end of the data transmission have components called transducers, which transform the data from digital data to light and back

Fiber optic cables transmit information for the Internet, telephone systems, and cable television.

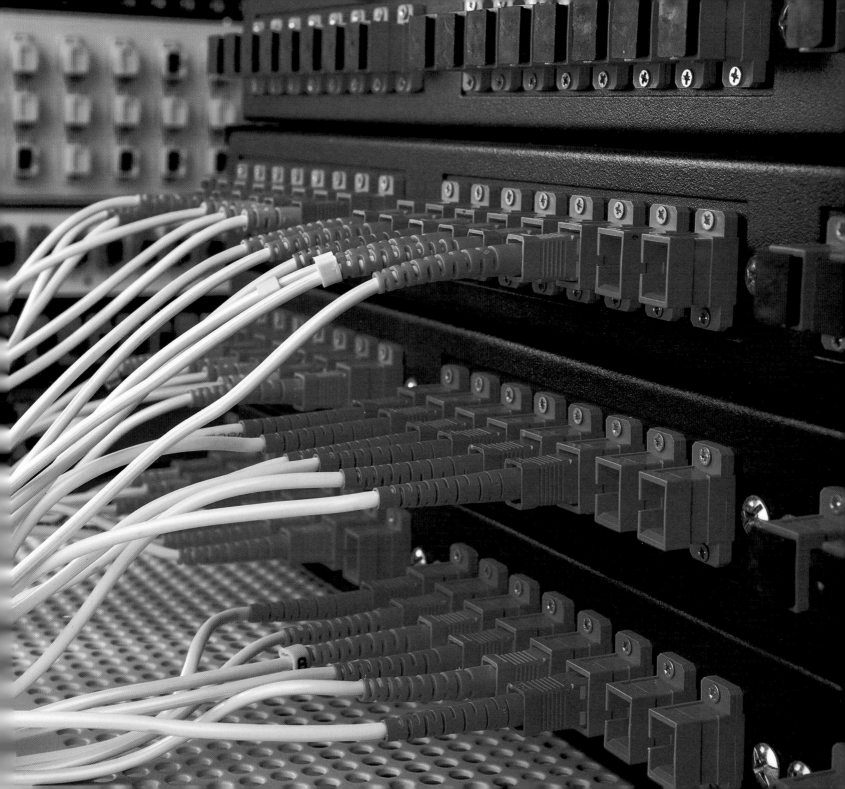

HOW PEOPLE SEE THE INTERNET

Kevin Kelly, a Silicon Valley philosopher, carried out an Internet Mapping Project in 2009. On his blog, he asked people to draw maps showing how they envisioned the Internet. Mara Vanina Osés, a psychologist and media professor at the University of Buenos Aires in Argentina, analyzed more than 50 of the drawings and created a system to organize people's visions. She found two major approaches. Some saw the Internet as a chaotic, spidery web reaching into infinity. Others portrayed the Internet as a village. No one included the machines that compose the Internet. Instead, they described it as a "landscape of the mind."[7]

again. Information traveling these fiber-optic cables eventually reaches more than 3 billion people, or approximately 39 percent of the world's population.[6]

Today's Internet represents an unsurpassed revolution in worldwide communication. It encompasses most important functions of the telegraph, telephone, radio, television, and computer. It allows us to broadcast worldwide, disseminate all forms of information, and connect and collaborate almost instantly with anyone the world over. Many individuals have made major contributions to Internet development. But more important, the Internet came about, and continues to evolve, because of collaboration.

Long, thin fiber-optic cables snake up to 15,000 miles (24,100 km) along the bottom of the ocean, carrying Internet information in the form of light from continent to continent.[8]

TIMELINE
THE INTERNET

1969
On October 29, Dr. Leonard Kleinrock oversees the sending of the first Internet message between the first two computers.

1973
The term *Internet* is born; Advanced Research Projects Agency Network (ARPANET) goes global.

1983
Finalized versions of two basic protocol programs, TCP and IP are introduced for ARPANET.

1983
The domain name system (DNS), a site naming system, is established. Domain names include .edu, .gov, .com, .mil, .org, .net, and .int.

1986
The National Science Foundation Network (NSFNET) connects ARPANET to academic users from research and educational institutions.

1990
Tim Berners-Lee develops hypertext markup language (HTML).

1991
The World Wide Web (WWW) goes public.

1993
The White House and the United Nations go online; NSFNET grows from 2,000 users in 1985 to more than 2 million in 1993.

1995
The Internet transitions from military and educational use to commercial use.

1998
The Google search engine is launched.

2001
Wikipedia goes online.

2004
Facebook, founded by Mark Zuckerberg, goes online; the Mozilla Firefox browser is launched.

2005
YouTube is launched.

2012
An online protest in January is mounted to stop two bills in Congress: the Stop Online Piracy Act (SOPA) and the PROTECT IP Act (PIPA).

2015
The Federal Communications Commission (FCC) passes new net neutrality laws.

CHAPTER 2

CREATING THE
INTERNET

The Internet had to be imagined before it could be created. In 1934, Belgian information expert Paul Otlet visualized what he called a radiated library, similar to today's Internet. It would have used the existing technology of radio and telephone. In 1945, Vannevar Bush, a government science adviser, published an article in the *Atlantic Monthly*. Bush proposed a device called a memex, which combined existing technology in new ways to enhance human memory. It would store information on microfilm and retrieve and connect it rapidly, using a keyboard, screen, buttons, and levers. Bush's memex concept captivated the thinking of many Internet developers. His proposed system was similar to

The US Army used early computers to store information and make calculations.

MURRAY LEINSTER'S "LOGIC"

Science fiction writers also envisioned a future Internet. In his 1946 story, *A Logic Named Joe*, Murray Leinster described a future in which everyone owned a system called a logic. This tabletop box had a screen, punch keys, and a videophone. People received information by connecting with a tank containing "all the facts in creation" and connected with other tanks around the country.[1] Although crude by modern standards, Leinster's vision had much in common with today's Internet.

hypertext, or computer text containing links to other text or to audio, video, or graphics.

Before the Internet, the military, the government, universities, and some businesses used computers for calculations and data management, but not for communication. Private individuals did not. Computers were excellent for making extremely rapid calculations with no errors, and at first, they were mostly replacements for hand-operated calculators. Governments and universities calculated designs for technologies such as airplanes. Businesses used them to process financial information. All programs and information storage were contained within each computer. To transfer information from one computer to another, programmers copied information onto discs and carried or mailed them to new locations. The ability to make rapid, accurate calculations was so new and exciting that, at first, only a few people considered connecting computers, and no one understood how it would change the ability to communicate.

ARPANET—The First Internet

The Internet finally came about because the Department of Defense (DOD) needed more reliable wartime communications. In the 1950s, the only means of communication was the telephone system. But telephones depended on switching stations, which were connecting points, or nodes, connecting the lines. Nodes could be attacked and knocked out, disrupting communications. The DOD wanted a weblike network system that could reroute communications around failed nodes. It wanted to use digital communications, or connected computers. The DOD also feared the rapid development of the Soviet space program. Finally, the DOD believed connected computers would make science researchers more efficient because they could share information rapidly.

The person who drove the development of the new DOD system was J. C. R. Licklider of the Massachusetts Institute of Technology (MIT). In October 1962, Licklider became the first head of the computer research program at the US Defense Department's Advanced Research Projects Agency (ARPA). In April 1963, he proposed a concept he whimsically dubbed the "intergalactic network."[2] Licklider envisioned a worldwide network of interconnected computers through which any user could access data and programs from any other computer—much like today's Internet. He convinced fellow MIT and ARPA researchers of the importance of his networking idea. Beginning in 1965, Lawrence Roberts and Thomas Marill, a former student of Licklider's, worked together to develop a plan for a computer

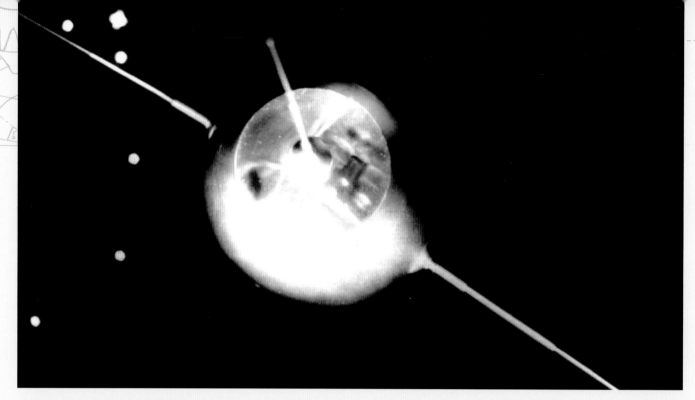

Launch of the *Sputnik* satellite in 1957 had shown that Soviet space technology was far ahead of US technology.

network. In 1969, the DOD commissioned and funded the development of this fledgling Internet, which they called Advanced Research Projects Agency Network (ARPANET).

Packet Switching and Extending of ARPANET

The major advance envisioned by Roberts, Marill, and others to be used in ARPANET was packet switching. This process allowed large masses of data to be broken down into packets, or small chunks. Packets moved easily through any part of a network and were reassembled at their final destination. Because packets could travel through any free space on the network, they could avoid bottlenecks and speed up information flow. Between 1961 and 1967, three groups of researchers had independently developed packet-switching technology: Leonard Kleinrock at MIT, Paul Baran and others at the RAND Corporation, and Donald Davies and Roger Scantlebury in the United Kingdom's National Physical Laboratory. The packet-switching devices were incorporated into the interface message processor (IMP). IMPs were the first routers.

ARPANET was formally launched at the end of 1969, when the nodes at UCLA and Stanford were joined by two more, at the University of California, Santa Barbara, and the University of Utah. Early ARPANET telephone lines were dedicated lines. They sent only ARPANET messages, not general ones; that is, a private person could not make a call on a dedicated line. The earliest ARPANET nodes were located at universities that were already ARPA sites with dedicated telephone lines. But for

REQUEST FOR COMMENTS

In 1969, ARPA tasked six graduate students with developing Internet communication protocols, called file transfer protocols (FTPs). These were the first programs that would tell connected computers how to transfer files across the new Internet. The students formed a loose network-working group with Steve Crocker, a student of Leonard Kleinrock, as unofficial leader. The group communicated by notes they called "Request for Comments" (RFCs). They sent the first RFCs as hard copies by regular mail, but as the new FTPs were developed, they were sent as online files. The humble, inviting tone of RFCs initiated an open, collaborative approach still used today by computer researchers.

The first four nodes forming ARPANET were located at the Stanford Research Institute (SRI); University of California, Los Angeles (UCLA); University of California, Santa Barbara (UCSB); and University of Utah (UTAH). Notations in the circles describe the type of computer at each location. The IMPs are the small computers that connect and translate digital information so it can be read by a different type of computer.

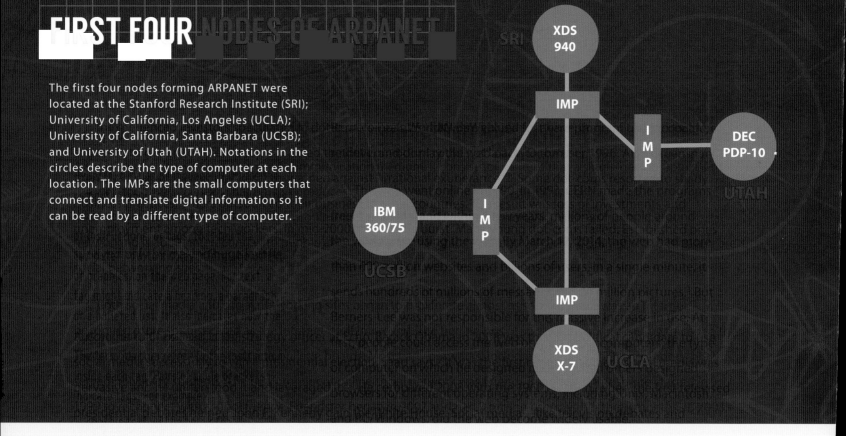

SRI
XDS 940
IMP

DEC PDP-10
I M P

UTAH

IBM 360/75
I M P

UCSB

IMP

XDS X-7
UCLA

ARPANET to expand, outside computers had to be able to dial directly into the network using ordinary telephone lines. In addition to IMPs, ARPANET accomplished this using small computers called terminal interface processors (TIPs), introduced in September 1971. TIPs allowed direct telephone connection of computer terminals—computer workstations separate from the main computer, where the user sends, receives, and views information from the computer. TIPs made it possible for individual users of a large computer to sit at their own desks and directly access the network. Thus, TIPs made distant connections much easier and sped up the addition of ARPANET nodes.

But continued growth of ARPANET required development of host-to-host protocols—software programs that allowed different types of computers to talk to each other. Before host-to-host protocols, different computer systems (and there were many) spoke different languages. There was no easy way for two different types of computers to exchange messages and ensure that no packets were lost or corrupted. Steve Crocker of UCLA directed development of the first ARPANET protocol program, the network control protocol (NCP), which was implemented during 1971 and 1972. The NCP was a program that provided step-by-step instructions for connecting two distant computers. This standardized the connection process and greatly decreased errors.

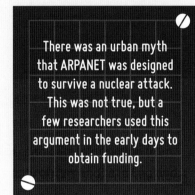

There was an urban myth that ARPANET was designed to survive a nuclear attack. This was not true, but a few researchers used this argument in the early days to obtain funding.

The original NCP worked with ARPANET, which communicated by landline telephones only. In May 1974, a group headed by Robert Kahn and Vint Cerf outlined a new protocol, called the transmission control protocol (TCP). TCP

THE SPREAD OF ARPANET

These two maps illustrate the spread of ARPANET throughout the United States. The left map shows ARPANET nodes in 1971; the right map shows them in 1983. ARPANET continued to add nodes until it was disbanded in 1990.

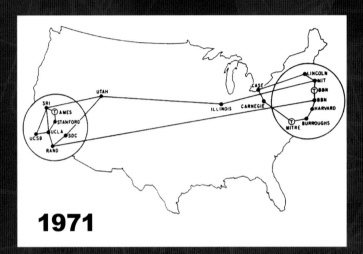

1971

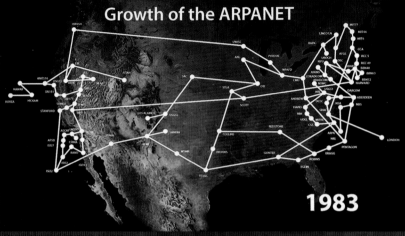

Growth of the ARPANET

1983

enabled communication through satellite and radio connections as well as landlines. It verified safe delivery of information packets, resent them if necessary, and controlled the direction and rate of information flow. TCP was much more flexible than NCP. It would allow the Internet to expand indefinitely around the globe.

TCP also had a second advantage. It took over the functions of the original dedicated computer, the IMP. This meant the system was controlled from the outside, by the individual computers connecting to it, rather than from the IMPs at the center. With the earlier NCP, the Internet was controlled through the IMP at each facility. This meant that, ultimately, the company that built the IMP controlled the network, because the company was responsible for updating, repairing, and monitoring it. Decentralized control of TCP made it easier to expand the network, because new computers or terminals could control their own addition. Later, to streamline its functions, TCP was divided into two parts: TCP, to handle communications between computers, and a new program, Internet protocol (IP), to handle interconnections between networks. This program, called TCP/IP, is still in use today.

With these innovations, ARPANET was able to expand. By the end of 1973, it had 37 sites, including satellite links from Hawaii, England, and Norway. By 1977, there were 111 sites, and by 1985, gateway sites existed throughout North America, Europe, and Australia.[3] But ARPANET was still a closed society. It included the military, universities, and related large businesses, but no individuals.

CHAPTER 3

INTERNET FOR EVERYONE

W ho exactly created the Internet? Was it the government because it financed ARPANET and the early advances that made today's Internet possible? Was it private-sector businesses, such as Apple and Xerox, whose innovations improved, enhanced, and commercialized the Internet? According to author Steven Johnson, the correct answer is neither. The worldwide expansion of the Internet came about because of vast, decentralized "peer networks" of computer enthusiasts. They developed thousands of Internet applications—not for pay, but because they were excited by the possibilities. Johnson says, "What sounds on the face of it like the most utopian of collectivist

Many people have worked to develop the Internet into the worldwide network it is today.

Major companies including IBM entered the personal computer business, commercializing computer and Internet use in the 1980s.

fantasies—millions of people sharing their ideas with no ownership claims—turns out to have made possible the communications infrastructure of our age."[1]

ARPANET lasted until 1990, but during its 20-year existence, new networks were formed and connected to it, and gradually, these specialized networks morphed into the Internet we know today. For those first 20 years,

Internet funding and use were limited primarily to defense organizations and universities. Even into the 1990s, many researchers assumed that only officials in government and academia would, or should, use the Internet. Agencies including the Department of Energy and National Aeronautics and Space Administration (NASA) and computer science researchers in academics and industry built early networks for specific purposes. In the 1980s, two networks were formed to serve members of college and university communities, regardless of their disciplines. These were Janet in the United Kingdom and the National Science Foundation Network (NSFNET) in the United States.

In 1983, ARPANET divided into two parts, ARPANET and MILNET, military network. ARPANET data remained public; MILNET transferred classified military information. In 1990, when ARPANET was retired, most university networks connected to it were moved to NSFNET. As these changes were occurring, many students and amateurs began seeing the implications of Internet use by the public. In addition to professionally written programs, unofficial applications developed by hobbyists began opening the Internet to everyone.

E-mail—An Early Application

As ARPANET developed and expanded through the 1970s and 1980s, its developers designed new computer hardware or improved existing hardware. Other developers created technology for connecting computers, including interface computers such as IMPs and TIPs. Many groups worked on application software. Applications, or apps, allow people to use the computer to do all the jobs they need to do. Every job a computer does requires an application. Applications are one of two general types of programs. The other type is system software, the programs required to run the computer itself. These programs run in the background; that is, the user is unaware of them. Applications are said to run on top of the system software. Manufacturers install and deliver system software with the computer. Application software is extra, although manufacturers usually include some applications as standard. The user can also choose and add more application programs.

One of the first Internet applications was introduced in 1972. First called electronic mail, it soon became just e-mail, and today it is hard to imagine the Internet without it. Ray Tomlinson of BBN (the company that developed IMPs) wrote the basic program to send and read e-mail. Lawrence Roberts expanded the software by adding basic commands that allowed the user to read, file, forward, and respond to messages. Although many essential applications, such as host-to-host protocols, were developed during ARPANET's 20-year existence, e-mail remained the largest Internet application for more than a decade and is still essential to most users.

Making Sharing Easier

A major impetus for early development of ARPANET and later the Internet was the need for resource sharing. Early computers were large, expensive, and far apart. Connecting them enabled sharing of all resources—hardware,

Ray Tomlinson helped create the e-mail program, including the use of the @ symbol used in each e-mail address.

WHAT DO I DO NOW?

In the early days, people outside the government were not sure what to do with an Internet connection. Cliff Stanford, the founder of Demon Internet, Britain's first commercial Internet service provider, says the main question his company received at the beginning was, "OK, I'm connected—what do I do now?"[2] According to Stanford, "We would answer with, 'Well, what do you want to do? Do you want to send an e-mail?'" People would answer, "I don't know anyone with an e-mail address."[3]

software, and information. Also, logging in remotely through a less expensive terminal workstation was much more economical than building a new mainframe computer at each location. E-mail had perhaps the greatest long-term effect. It completely changed the nature of communication and collaboration. Its speed and usefulness became obvious as people collaborated during the building of the Internet itself, and they quickly grasped its implications for communication in society more broadly.

One early advance that made resource sharing easier was setting up certain computers to act as servers. Any computer can be a server, as long as it has enough data storage space and memory for carrying out applications. Different types of servers run software suited to a particular type of application. For example, a file server uses a program that allows file sharing over the Internet. A web server provides access to websites. An e-mail server sends and receives e-mail.

Also, from the beginning, researchers gave every computer a unique identifier, an IP address. Because every IP address was unique, entering it as a destination ensured that data sent over the Internet would go to the correct computer. The structure of the IP address was defined by the TCP/IP protocol that outlined how to communicate on the Internet. An IP address consists of four numbers separated by decimal points. Each number ranges from 0 to 255. An example of a typical IP address is 212.55.6.186. Until 1983, all IP addresses were stored in a master file on a single server located at Stanford Research Institute (SRI). When users needed an address, they had to obtain it from this file by calling SRI during business hours.

As additional networks were added and the Internet increased in size, the naming system became more difficult to manage. Numeric IP addresses were difficult to remember. Also, each new network was managed independently, so it no longer made sense to have a single file of host IP addresses. Paul Mockapetris, of the University of Southern California, solved these issues by developing the domain name system (DNS). In the DNS, each computer is given an easy-to-remember alphabetic name—for example, "mycomputer.com." The DNS automated the naming system, so anyone with a connected computer could locate another computer by simply typing in its name, rather than its numeric IP address. Finally, it allowed people to update their own networks and have those changes visible to everyone else. Mockapetris's DNS went online in 1983 and was revised in 1986. The process for locating another computer on the Internet remains basically the same today.

WHAT IS A DOMAIN NAME?

Every domain name (and its associated IP address) is precise and unique, like an international telephone number for the Internet. Domain names refer to a series of specific computer servers. To reach a given Internet location—say a website—the DNS server first finds the most general server to which the domain name points. Then, it finds each more specific server, until it reaches the exact server containing the file requested. Suppose a domain name is:

mylifestory.mycomputer.net

The most general part of the name ("net") is at right. "Mycomputer" is more specific, and "mylifestory" is the most specific part of the name. The DNS server first locates the "net" server, which leads it to the "mycomputer" server, which in turn leads it to the "mylifestory" server, where the requested information is actually stored. The DNS connects this computer to the home computer.

Every website, e-mail address, or other application on the Internet is located on a computer somewhere. At various places around the Internet are specific DNS servers that store the locations of these computers. When a user connects to the Internet, the router that assigns the home computer's network IP address also assigns it a DNS server. It uses the DNS server to find the locations of domain names that the user types in. If that DNS server cannot find the correct computer, it contacts another DNS server, and so on, until it matches the address with the computer. When the Internet first began in the 1970s, all IP addresses could be contained in the single SRI file. Today, there are billions of IP addresses, each with its unique name.[4] All DNS servers process billions of location requests every day.[5]

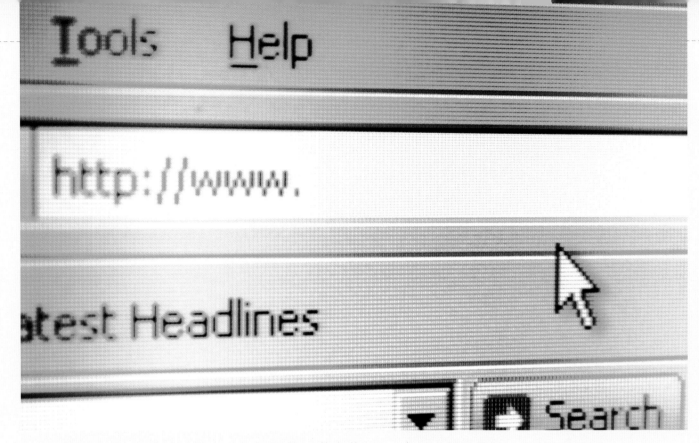

The DNS translates each name into a numeric IP address that other computers can recognize.

Open Access and E-mail Build the Internet

The entire history of Internet development has been based on open access. All documents relating to Internet development, beginning in 1969, are free and accessible to everyone on the Internet. These include documents describing protocols, technical standards, and engineering ideas. Entrepreneurs designing new software use them in

A person typing in a domain name is asking for directions to a specific computer. The home computer sends the request to the DNS server specified by its own network connection. This server either sends back the address or, if necessary, sends the request on to another DNS server. When the address is located, the user's computer uses the address to go to the appropriate computer.

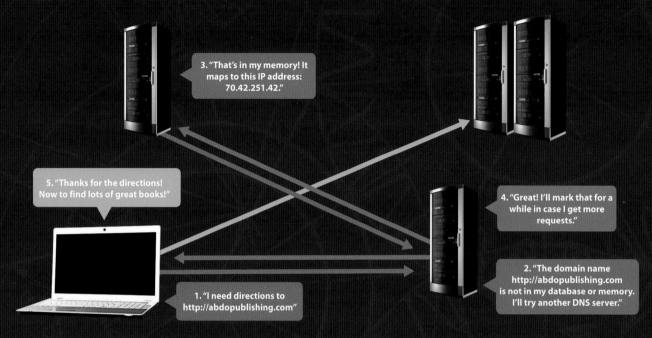

3. "That's in my memory! It maps to this IP address: 70.42.251.42."

5. "Thanks for the directions! Now to find lots of great books!"

4. "Great! I'll mark that for a while in case I get more requests."

2. "The domain name http://abdopublishing.com is not in my database or memory. I'll try another DNS server."

1. "I need directions to http://abdopublishing.com"

college classes. The open access approach has resulted in a decentralized Internet organization with no central controlling body. Instead, groups of people all over the world work together, share their results with other groups, and implement whatever programs seem worthwhile.

When Internet growth began taking off in the late 1970s, Vint Cerf and other pioneers recognized the need for better coordination and management of standards and technology. Maintaining the same community-based approach, they formed several worldwide coordinating bodies, with a working group for each research area. Researchers have now developed as many as 75 working groups for different topics.[6] Members of each group may be anywhere in the world. They are connected by an e-mail list and carry out discussions by e-mail.

Internet Service Providers

In the 1980s and 1990s, personal computers (PCs) became smaller, cheaper, and easier to use. Soon, they were available to individuals. Many computer owners immediately wanted to connect to the Internet. This resulted in the rise of Internet service providers (ISPs). These servers run programs that connect individual computers to the Internet. When an individual computer connects to the ISP's computers, software on the computer (in today's terms, a web browser) locates the Internet and connects the user with it.

At first, ISPs offered telephone dial-up connections to the Internet. The earliest service, called the Source, allowed people to access text data. It lasted from 1979 to 1989. It had a start-up cost of $100 and hourly rates higher than the minimum wage of the time.[7] CompuServe went online in 1989. It served businesses and techies, and later, the general

public. As competitors appeared, CompuServe went from hourly to flat monthly rates. AOL soon became the go-to ISP for new computer users because of its low monthly rates, online games, chat rooms, and instant messaging.

These early dial-up telephone connections were economical, but very slow and of low quality. The ISP provided the user with a telephone number. The user connected a modem to the PC, and the computer dialed the phone number to connect to the Internet. If the home had only one telephone line, this meant no one in the home could make or receive telephone calls while the Internet was in use. Today, slow dial-up telephone connections have mostly been replaced by much faster, high-quality digital broadband connections, such as cable and DSL.

Although the Internet originated as a specialized and closed technology used primarily by military and university researchers, it has evolved into something much different. The very act of connecting computers led early users to imagine the vast implications of connecting people, their work, and their ideas. The ease of communication begun by e-mail led to an explosion of cooperation and sharing, fueled by the open-access philosophy. Rapidly expanding technologies combined with an insistence on sharing has led to the Internet of today—truly an Internet for all.

Dial-up telephone connections still exist. The tech site Pingdom tested the time it took to load the top 50 websites using dial-up. Average load time was 105 seconds.[8]

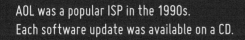

AOL was a popular ISP in the 1990s. Each software update was available on a CD.

PEER-TO-PEER FILE SHARING

Peer-to-peer (P2P) file sharing involves directly transferring files from one computer to another without going through a server. A special P2P software program is installed on all computers that are sharing files. The file is stored in a folder on the sending computer and uploaded, using the software, to a folder on the receiving computer. All users contribute their computer power and bandwidth to the process. Thus, the more computers involved in the P2P file distribution, the faster and more efficient the transfer process will be.

Early P2P systems were developed to share information among computer scientists working on new computer operating systems. One of these was Usenet, developed in 1979. Internet users quickly hijacked the concept to share music, videos, software, and photos.

P2P networks have new software programs that can be downloaded free, and millions of people use them to share music, videos, and movies. Detractors are concerned because P2P software not only enables downloading of copyrighted material but also risks downloading malware onto users' computers. New versions are difficult to block and to track.

A makes available a copy of the file in the specified folder and is uploading different parts of the file to B and C respectively.

INTERNET

C is downloading different parts of the file from A and B.

B is downloading part of the file from A and at the same time uploading to C the other part of the file that has been downloaded from A.

CHAPTER 4

CHANGING THE
WORLD

The Internet application that has had the most profound effect on society is the World Wide Web, now known simply as the web. Many people use the terms *Internet* and *web* interchangeably, but they are distinct. The Internet is the basic structure—the network of networks connecting computers all over the world. Its infrastructure is contained in a massive worldwide grid of fiber-optic cables.

The web allows users to access and share information over the Internet. Web information is contained in documents called web pages. Web pages are connected by hyperlinks and stored on

Tim Berners-Lee helped speed up worldwide communication with the invention of the World Wide Web in 1989.

web servers. Users access them through programs called web browsers, such as Microsoft Internet Explorer or Mozilla Firefox. The web is just one part of the Internet. Other methods of transmitting information over the Internet that are not part of the web include e-mail, instant messaging, Usenet news groups, and FTP sites. Each method relies on its own Internet language. For example, e-mail uses the language simple mail transfer protocol (SMTP).

Origin and Rise of the Web

The web originated in 1989 at CERN, now the European Laboratory for Particle Physics, near Geneva, Switzerland. Tim Berners-Lee, a British computer scientist, saw a need for more rapid communication among CERN scientists and other scientists around the world. He wrote a proposal for "a simple scheme to incorporate several different servers of machine-stored information already available at CERN."[1] He proposed using hypertext to link this information, so any piece of data would be accessible from any other. Types of information he wanted to link included reports, notes, databases, computer documentation, and online help. Berners-Lee's hypertext concept for ordering and using information efficiently owed much to the memex concept outlined by Vannevar Bush in 1945 and to a failed project by Internet philosopher Ted Nelson. Nelson's project,

Mathematicians calculated that the electrons in all the tubes of the Internet weigh approximately 1.8 ounces (50 g).[2] Thus, the information carried by the Internet and web weighs as much as a strawberry.

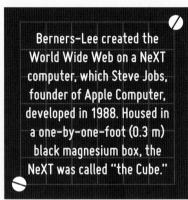

Berners-Lee created the World Wide Web on a NeXT computer, which Steve Jobs, founder of Apple Computer, developed in 1988. Housed in a one-by-one-foot (0.3 m) black magnesium box, the NeXT was called "the Cube."

begun around 1965, also linked documents using hypertext. But Berners-Lee's web concept quickly became dominant, primarily because he wrote specific programs to implement it.

To make his proposal a reality, Berners-Lee designed three application programs: the hypertext transfer protocol (HTTP), the hypertext markup language (HTML), and the world's first web browser, which he named WorldWideWeb (WWW). Together, HTTP and HTML are the programs that control how the web functions. HTTP consists of commands that define how to format and transmit messages and control how web servers and browsers respond to various commands. HTML controls the formatting and display of web pages. A web browser, such as

TIMOTHY BERNERS-LEE

In 1976, Timothy Berners-Lee graduated from The Queen's College in Oxford, England. He went to CERN as a software engineer in 1984. In 1989, he proposed the idea for the World Wide Web. The following year, he wrote the software, and the web went online. He now holds joint appointments as professor at MIT and the University of Southampton, England. He is a director of the World Wide Web Consortium (W3C), an organization that develops standards and protocols to ensure the growth of the web, and of the World Wide Web Foundation, which promotes use of the web to benefit humanity.

WHAT IS HTML?

Hypertext markup language (HTML) is the computer language used to design websites. When using HTML, the writer lists a series of instructions, or tags, that tell the computer how to display information (text or graphics) on the web page. For text, a tag might indicate a heading, a paragraph, or a bulleted list. It also indicates how the text will look, for example, bold or italic. The term *markup* refers to the instruction inside each tag. Pairs of angle brackets indicate tags. For example:

<b>This text will be bold.</b>

<title>This Is a Title.</title>

<p>This is a paragraph. It has several sentences.</p>

Berners-Lee's WorldWideWeb, is a software program used to locate, retrieve, and display the web page to the user.

The web went online in 1990. In 1993, CERN made the programs freely available, and within a few years, millions of people around the world were using the web. By March 12, 2014, the web had more than 600 million websites and billions of users. In a single minute, it sends hundreds of millions of messages and 20 million pictures.[3] But Berners-Lee was not responsible for this massive increase in use. At first, people could access the web only on NeXT computers, the type of computer on which he designed it. Only when others designed browsers for different operating systems, including Unix, Macintosh, and PC/Windows, did the web become widely usable.

The number of network connections exploded, reaching 6.6 million computers by July 1995 and 19.6 million only two years later.[4] Web software had made the Internet easy to use, and web users quickly

Early webcams were also used to watch weather to determine if it was safe to fly airplanes.

found new ways to use it. An early application was the webcam, invented at the University of Cambridge in England. Webcams quickly became popular, so that anyone with an Internet connection could view traffic jams, life in college dorms, and zoo animals.

Perhaps because it is both friendly and easy to use, Yahoo! still exists today.

Finding Information: The Search Engine

As websites began proliferating in the early 1990s, it became harder for users to find the sites they wanted. Browser search capabilities were limited, and it was difficult to find a specific website unless the user knew in advance what to look for. Enter a new type of software—the search engine. A browser gets the user onto the web, and a search engine locates specific websites. The search engine sends out a web crawler or spider—a program that copies and indexes all the web pages it finds. When indexing, a web crawler finds and stores a list of keywords from every page on every website it searches. When the user sends a query to the search engine, it sorts these keywords to find websites that match keywords in the query.

One of the earliest search engines was a web crawler called Wanderer, which was introduced in 1993. It pioneered two features that became standard in later search engines: it was the first web crawler, and it indexed the data. Four other search engines were also introduced in 1993: AltaVista, Lycos, Yahoo!, and Excite. Yahoo! included links to its competitors' websites so the user could compare searches. But the web search really came into its own in the late 1990s with the introduction of a radical new search engine called Google.

CHAPTER 5

SEARCH ENGINES

Today's teens never knew life without Google. It is now so pervasive that the word is no longer only the name of a software program. It is a verb—when anyone needs information about anything, the automatic response is, "Just Google it." But Google is a relatively new search engine. Founders Larry Page and Sergey Brin only formed the company in 1998. Perhaps it revolutionized society so quickly because these inventors did not think small. According to Page, "Basically, our goal is to organize the world's information and to make it universally accessible and useful."[1]

Larry Page and Sergey Brin started Google in the 1990s from their dorm room at Stanford University.

The Founding of Google

Page and Brin became friends and collaborators as graduate students at Stanford University in 1996. Page had gained fame as an undergraduate at the University of Michigan by building an inkjet printer from Lego® blocks. Brin had been an honors student in mathematics and computer science at the University of Maryland. At Stanford, the two began by working together on Page's BackRub research project. This project explored "backlinks," or links that referred back to other websites as a way to determine the relative importance of a site. Based on this information, they developed the PageRank algorithm, which they thought would provide better search results than searches based only on the number of times a search term appeared. They worked from their dorm rooms, using Stanford servers. Their project quickly developed into the search site Google.com.

The name "Google" comes from the word *googol*, which is the number 1 followed by 100 zeroes. This gigantic number suggests Google's attempt to organize the seemingly infinite amount of information on the web.

As Google's popularity increased, Page and Brin ran out of computer power and began to beg for computers. In mid-1998, with their site getting 10,000 searches per day, they maxed out their credit cards to start a company, and Google was incorporated on September 4, 1998.[2] In December of the same year, *PC Magazine* recognized Google as one of the 100 best websites of 1998 and "the search engine of choice," stating that it "has an uncanny knack for returning extremely relevant results."[3]

Google's headquarters, the Googleplex, located in Mountain View, California, is a huge, growing campus with more than 11,000 employees.

Google grew rapidly. In May 2000, it released the first ten language versions of Google (today, searches can be done in more than 150 languages). In rapid succession, new specific search programs were launched—including Google Images in 2001, Google News and Froogle in 2002, and Google Print (now Google Books) in 2003. The company went public in 2004.[4] By 2013, Google's revenue was $15.7 billion.[5]

Cloud Computing and Web 2.0

Google quickly became recognized as the web's best search engine. Part of its success is due to cloud computing, or the storage of user data on huge Internet servers instead of on the user's PC. Cloud computing and Google developed in parallel during the late 1990s and 2000s. Although the cloud-computing concept arose in the 1960s, it only became practical in the late 1990s, when high-speed Internet service became available. Cloud computing began as a service for companies with lots of data to store rather than individuals. In 2002, Amazon Web Services pioneered cloud-based services to customers, including storage and computation. Amazon's Elastic Compute Cloud (E2C), launched in 2006, became the first widely accessible cloud computing service. Then, late in the decade, Web 2.0 rose to prominence. This second generation of the World Wide Web gave people a much greater ability to collaborate and share information online—thanks to cloud computing.

Cloud computing gives users much more freedom. Because their data is stored on the Internet, people are not tied to their own computers. They can access data from any connected computer. Huge servers can store almost unlimited amounts of data. Because the cloud also contains software, users can create documents and otherwise manipulate data. They can collaborate on shared projects, with different people updating the same document in real time.

Some people worry about security and privacy on the cloud. Cloud computing companies must be able to keep stored data safe, or they will quickly lose clients. Privacy is more difficult, because users can log in from anywhere. To prevent unauthorized access, users must employ authentication techniques, such as names and passwords.

Just Google It!

To search the world's ever-expanding mass of data, Google relies on complex algorithms. Google's algorithms help users find the most relevant information quickly—not only text, but also images, news, videos, and maps.

Throughout its more than 15 years of existence, Google has continued building new tools. Its new products help people find information as well as work and communicate more efficiently. Google tools are easy to use, and they run on any computer with a web browser and an Internet connection. They are free to users because the company makes money

GOOGLE'S SEARCH ALGORITHMS

Google's algorithms use more than 200 clues, such as terms on websites, date of content, and user's location, to determine more precisely what a user is looking for.[6] Although Google's algorithms are kept secret, its searches are based on a ranking system. Google remembers and ranks information from previous searches and uses it to sort websites so the most relevant sites appear first in the search results.

by selling advertising space. Popular tools include Google Maps, Google News, Gmail, Google Docs, and YouTube, which Google bought in 2006.

Google has made research faster and more efficient. It has given people access to greater quantities of information than ever before. PBS writer Jennifer Woodard Maderazo says Google has made people impatient and "spoiled for instant information gratification."[7] They no longer enjoy a leisurely search for knowledge, such as wandering through a library or poring over an encyclopedia, finding unexpected but fascinating topics. A 2012 study even suggests the human mind is changing so it remembers how to find information without remembering the information itself.[8]

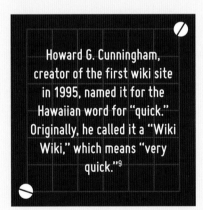

Howard G. Cunningham, creator of the first wiki site in 1995, named it for the Hawaiian word for "quick." Originally, he called it a "Wiki Wiki," which means "very quick."[9]

What Is a Wiki?

If Google has changed the way people find information, the wiki has changed the way we learn and teach. A wiki is a collaborative website where several authors enter and change information continuously. Once an author places content on a wiki site, anyone with a browser and access to that site can edit, delete, or change it. Wikis are a prime example of the use of Web 2.0. Because wikis are designed to accommodate multiple authors, they are helpful for large projects. Students doing a class project, teachers designing a new curriculum, industry professionals

Google uses a special car to create the "Street View" element on Google Maps.

developing a business plan, writers collaborating on a book—any of these groups might use a wiki.

Wikis enable collaborators to jot down ideas so they will not be lost. They allow instant communication, and they serve as archives, because they retain every version of a document. But wikis can be messy. They

GOOGLE MAPS

Google Maps began with Google Earth. This tool, which views Earth from above, combines satellite imagery with ground-level geographic information, allowing the user to zoom in on any spot on Earth. It connects the map imagery with news, photos, and other information useful to travelers, students, and the public. Google Maps is a down-to-earth, practical version of Google Earth. Its mapping software provides users with addresses, directions, and information about landmarks. Google Sky combines satellite data, surface photography, and astronomy data, enabling exploration of the night sky and solar system. New tools use Google Earth technology to provide close-up views of the moon and Mars.

require collaborators to understand a simplified markup language, similar to HTML. Unless well managed, wikis work best with a small number of collaborators.

The Rise of Wikipedia

The online encyclopedia Wikipedia is the largest and best-known example of a wiki. Wikipedia was launched in January 2001. By February 2010, it contained 14.4 million articles, 3.2 million of them in English.[10] Earlier online encyclopedias contained peer-reviewed articles, written and reviewed by experts. Wikipedia is an open-content encyclopedia, with articles written by volunteers. But, because editing is also free and open to all, editors can quickly correct or remove inaccurate content.

Jimmy Wales and Larry Sanger founded Wikipedia. Wales received two degrees in finance, a bachelor's degree from Auburn University in Alabama and a master's degree from the University of Alabama. Wales became an Internet entrepreneur and hired Sanger to manage his online encyclopedia, Nupedia, which was written by experts and funded by ads. Sanger had a PhD in philosophy from Ohio State University. Sanger suggested the wiki approach and the name, and the two started Wikipedia as a side project. It was ad-free and written by volunteers rather than experts. Wikipedia quickly overtook Nupedia and went global.

Jimmy Wales came up with the original concept for Wikipedia.

According to its policy, Wikipedia "is an encyclopedia. Its goals go no further."[11] Its articles cannot contain personal essays, opinions, critical reviews, propaganda, or original research. It simply catalogs what has already been learned. All Wikipedia articles should have a neutral viewpoint and objectively present differing views of a subject. Wikipedia authors should never plagiarize from other authors, on the web or elsewhere.

Wikipedia's articles are entirely free for anyone to read. Most scholarly journal articles, in contrast, can only be accessed after paying a large subscription fee. Wikipedia articles are also free for anyone to use on websites or in books, as long as their use is not restricted. Finally, Wikipedia is collaborative. Every article has multiple, unnamed authors.

Why Will My Teacher Not Let Me Use Wikipedia?

In 2008, a professor in the United Kingdom banned her students from using either Google or Wikipedia in their research projects. She stated that students "don't come to university to learn how to Google."[12] Like Google, Wikipedia tends to make researchers lazy, depending on the easiest and quickest source, rather than digging deeper and checking original sources.

But what makes educators most wary of using Wikipedia is that experts do not write it. According to OnlineCollegeCourses.com, "Even Wikipedia founder Jimmy Wales doesn't think of his creation as a viable academic resource."[13] Many pages are excellent and completely accurate, but Wikipedia's open nature makes it vulnerable to uninformed contributors, poor writing, and so-called trolls who deliberately abuse the system.

By early 2015, Wikipedia had more than 4.7 million English articles, with more than 800 new articles added every day.

WIKIPEDIA

English
The Free Encyclopedia
3 571 000+ articles

日本語
フリー百科事典
736 000+ 記事

Deutsch
Die freie Enzyklopädie
1 196 000+ Artikel

Español
La enciclopedia libre
728 000+ artículos

Français
L'encyclopédie libre
1 073 000+ articles

Русский
Свободная энциклопедия
679 000+ статей

Italiano
L'enciclopedia libera
778 000+ voci

Português
A enciclopédia livre
674 000+ artigos

Nederlands
De vrije encyclopedie
674 000+ artikelen

Polski
Wolna encyklopedia
779 000+ haseł

suchen · rechercher · szukaj · ricerca · 検索 · buscar · поиск · busca · zoeken · sök · 검색
tìm kiếm · 찾기 · căutare · ara · cari · seg · 검색
hledání · keresés · Пошук · cari · poišči · bilinga

CHAPTER 6

SOCIAL SITES

Today, social networking is a part of everyday life. The Internet and web began this transformation, but much of it is possible because of mobile phones and Wi-Fi. Other mobile devices, including iPods, MP3 players, and even automobile GPS units, are also helping turn society into what sociologists Scott Campbell and Yong Jin Park describe as the "personal communication society."[1]

Cell Phone History

The cell phone turned 40 years old in 2013. During that time, it has undergone an incredible transformation. Cell phone designer Martin Cooper of Motorola Labs made the first cell phone call on

tagram

Share
Moments

ok

Welcome to Facebook – Log In, Sign Up or Learn More

Pinterest

Pinterest

Linked in.

Email or Phone

☑ Keep me logged in

Password

Forgot your passw

Google+

WhatsApp

Social media sites are the vehicles by which teens and most adults in many parts of the world communicate with friends and family.

THE FIRST SMARTPHONES

A prototype of the first smartphone, the IBM Simon Personal Communicator was developed in 1992, and two years later, BellSouth Cellular made it available to the public. The Simon was a cellphone with personal digital assistant (PDA) features, including a calendar, clock, and appointment scheduler. It could send and receive e-mails, exchange faxes, and run some applications. BellSouth discontinued it in 1995. The term *smartphone* had not been invented when the Simon was released. The first phone described as a smartphone was the Erickson R380, released in 2000. It was similar in size and weight to a typical cell phone and had many organizer functions, a data port, and e-mail and Internet access, but no additional apps could be installed.

April 3, 1973, on the streets of New York City. Cooper phoned his rival, Joel Engel of Bell Labs, using a cell phone that was 10 inches (25.4 cm) long and weighed 2.5 pounds (1.13 kg). This was ten times the weight of the iPhone 5, released in 2013.[2] Many of the earliest cell phones were considered car phones because they were too heavy and bulky to carry.

In 1982, the Federal Communications Commission (FCC) approved formation of a mobile telephone system. The first cell phone available to the public—the Motorola DynaTAC, nicknamed "the brick"— debuted in 1983. It cost $3,995 (more than $8,700 at 2014 prices).[3] Through the years, cell phones have drastically decreased in size and price while increasing in abilities. Early phones were mostly used in sales and business, rather than by individuals. Soon, manufacturers realized their phones could do more than talk. They added functions such as address books, e-mail, and paging. IBM's Simon Personal Communicator, from 1994, was the first to have such smartphone capabilities, and it cost less than $1,000.[4] The Motorola Razr V3, released in 2004, was the first ultrathin phone. Apple released the first iPhone in 2007.

Cell Phones, Wi-Fi, and Smartphones

Cell phones freed people from the home or office and enabled them to make telephone calls on the move. But, until the 1990s, they could access the Internet only from a fixed location—by plugging a cable into a computer or laptop. Not until the advent of Wi-Fi technology were people able to reach the Internet from nearly anywhere. In 1985, the FCC designated three bands of radio waves for the use of wireless technology. This led to the development of wireless local area networks, or WLANs, more commonly known as Wi-Fi or wireless Internet. A WLAN is a small wireless network operating within a relatively confined space—a home, coffee shop, or airline terminal, for instance. People within range of the WLAN can connect to the Internet without cables or telephone lines.

The Institute of Electrical and Electronics Engineers (IEEE) manages development of Wi-Fi technology. Wi-Fi technology advanced through several versions during the 1990s, gradually overcoming difficulties with speed, range, and interference from other electronics.

HOW CELL PHONES AND WI-FI WORK

Cell phones consist of a combined radio transmitter and receiver. The cell phone transforms a sender's voice into electric signals, which travel as radio waves. The receiver's phone converts the radio waves back into sound. Similar to a walkie-talkie, the technology has a very short range of transmission. Setting up a network increases the range. Land area is divided into sections called cells, each with its own base station, a cell tower or set of antennas linking cell phones to the wireless network. A cell phone signal is transmitted from one base station to another until it reaches its destination. A Wi-Fi transmitter receives Internet information, converts it into a radio signal, and sends it. Computers in the WLAN receive the radio signals through a wireless adapter. The computers or cell phones send information to the wireless transmitter, which converts and sends signals across the broadband connection.

At first, many people owned two separate devices. The cell phone made telephone calls, but did nothing else. The personal digital assistant (PDA) stored contact information, kept schedules, and linked with the owner's computer. More advanced PDAs had Internet access and could send and receive e-mail. As the smartphone began combining the functions of these two devices, the PDA became unnecessary.

Combining cell phone and Wi-Fi technologies produced Wi-Fi cell phones, which automatically switch between the two technologies when the caller is within a Wi-Fi signal area. This helps prevent dropped or lost calls. It also added Internet capabilities to the cell phone, opening up a world of new possibilities for mobile devices. The first Wi-Fi certified cell phone was introduced in 2004, and today Wi-Fi is a common feature on smartphones. In addition to telephone capabilities, still and video cameras, and a touch keyboard, today's typical smartphones have computer

Cell phones affect how people coordinate their daily activities and lifestyles.

operating systems for downloading and running applications. They have apps, can send and receive text messages, and synchronize, or sync, with the user's e-mail accounts. Smartphone capabilities change rapidly, and next year's smartphone will likely be much smarter than this year's version.

Mobile Phones and Communication

Spanish sociologist Manuel Castells says the recent explosion of mobile devices has helped to nourish the rise of a "network society." According to Castells, flow of information through the Internet has helped make social organization more decentralized, flexible, and "based on shared interests rather than shared geographic space."[5] He does not think the new technology is actually causing the change in social order; it is simply stimulating a change already occurring in society.

The smartphone has been a major driver in the formation of the network society. According to sociologists Scott W. Campbell and Yong Jin Park, smartphones have affected society in four ways. They have changed the relationship between technology and the human body. Smartphones have also changed people's personal use of public space. And they have led to the rise of a mobile youth culture.

The smartphone has definitely changed the human body/technology relationship. Modern computers and tablets are relatively small and portable, but communication over these devices, for example by e-mail or Skype, requires sitting in front of them. The much smaller smartphone is portable and wearable; it is an extension of self that expresses a person's fashion sense and social status.

The smartphone has changed lifestyles. People can make and change plans anywhere and any time. They can maintain constant contact with friends and family, texting or calling each other many times a day, just to keep in touch. If a child is late getting home, a mother can call to ask "Where are you?" This constant communication strengthens the bonds of family and friendship, according to Campbell and Park. Friendships are not restricted only to those people in the immediate vicinity; friendships can develop—and be maintained—with people at a distance. In the "personal communication society," more personal conversations occur in public spaces.[6] This has changed the boundaries of what society considers appropriate. To many parents and grandparents, telephone conversations should be private. But bystanders are now frequently forced to overhear private conversations. Personal activities once carried out in the privacy of one's own home are now carried out in public. Should society make rules? Where should we allow cell phones, and where should we ban them? These questions are new, and no firm conventions are yet in place.

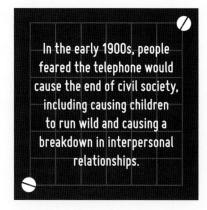

In the early 1900s, people feared the telephone would cause the end of civil society, including causing children to run wild and causing a breakdown in interpersonal relationships.

People of all ages now use smartphones, but youth have adopted the practice to such an extent that sociologists now speak of the "mobile youth culture."[7] Young people are more tolerant of the distractions of smartphones in their public spaces. Smartphones are almost essential for maintaining relationships and planning social activities. Young people are constantly connected. They have more freedom in personal relationships and more privacy from parents. And the mobile society is quickly evolving to encompass all generations.

History of Social Media and Social Networking

A social media site is a "one-to-many" communication medium. It consists of content that a single person uploads to the web for others to view. That person produces and owns the content and viewers can comment on it. On a social networking site, a user creates a public profile and forms relationships with others who have access to the site. Social networking is about interacting with people and creating relationships. Facebook, Twitter, Instagram, and Pinterest are social networking sites.

Both social media and social networking sites began to proliferate almost as soon as there was an Internet, becoming more sophisticated as the Internet itself improved. The beginnings of social networking can be traced to the 1970s, with the advent of e-mail and bulletin boards. Most early networks, including Usenet (1979) and Tripod (1992), served university students. The first prominent online social network was Friends Reunited, a British site started in 1999 to reconnect with school friends. Friendster began in 2002 and had 3 million users within three months. In 2003, MySpace began as an offshoot of Friendster. In 2004, Facebook was launched for students at Harvard College; in 2006 it was opened to all. Twitter was launched in 2006. It quickly took off, gaining 255 million users by 2014. Facebook remained the largest networking site, reaching 1.28 billion users in 2014. More than 6 billion of the world's 7.1 billion people have Internet access, and three-fourths of those use some form of social networking.[8]

Social media has followed a similar chronology. It took off with the introduction of the World Wide Web in 1993. GeoCities, which allowed users to create their own websites, began in 1994 and had more than 38 million users when it ceased US operations in 2009.[9] The first blogs began in 1997, Wikipedia in 2001, and Apple iTunes in 2003. In 2004, Flickr for image hosting began and Digg for sharing news stories went online. YouTube began in 2005 as a media outlet for storing and retrieving videos.

Effects of Social Networking and Social Media

There is no doubt these sites profoundly affect society and relationships. But is the effect good or bad? According to Brooke Foucault Welles, assistant professor of communication studies at the University of Chicago, it is usually good. People are becoming more dependent on social sites, but this is not necessarily negative.

TOP TEN SOCIAL MEDIA AND NETWORKING SITES

According to eBiz, the following sites were the most popular social media and networking sites in January 2015. Numbers represent counts of unique monthly visitors.

- Facebook (900,000,000)
- Twitter (310,000,000)
- LinkedIn (255,000,000)
- Pinterest (250,000,000)
- Google+ (120,000,000)
- Tumblr (110,000,000)
- Instagram (100,000,000)
- VK (80,000,000)
- Flickr (65,000,000)
- Vine (42,000,000)[10]

By 2014, YouTube had 540 million users.

Sociologist Barry Wellman agrees. "Online communication—e-mail, instant messaging, chat rooms, etc.—does not replace more traditional offline forms of contact—face-to-face and telephone. Instead, it adds on to them, increasing the overall volume of contact," Wellman said.[11] People use social media to make plans with people they already know.

But nearly every advantage of social media and networking sites has a corresponding downside. Although the sites spread information very rapidly, some information is inaccurate and even false, and this false information is also spread more rapidly. Law enforcement uses the sites to catch criminals. However, stalkers and other violent criminals may use these sites to find and lure victims. Some sites promote cyberbullying, hate groups, or child endangerment. Whereas some sites give important health and safety information, others disseminate inaccurate, amateur, and even dangerous advice. And although students can use these sites to discuss school-related work and do better in school, they may also perform poorly because they waste time or use social networking sites while studying. Social networks also decrease privacy by digitally recording social interactions. Although these vast information databases can be used for good—for example, to study social behaviors such as voting or the spread of diseases—no one can really predict how this information will be used or how it will affect future society.

In the 2000s, methods of communication are evolving rapidly. Technologies unimaginable even a generation ago are ordinary today, and people appear to be evolving with their new technology. Just as in past generations, all new technologies offer vast new possibilities for society, and it is up to people to use them wisely.

CHAPTER 7

BUSINESS AND POLITICS

You Tube

Radio Vaticana

Centro Televisivo Vaticano

Vatican.va

Vatican State

The Vatican

va
Sty
Joir
Las
Sub
Cha

DIRECTOR

Questo canale offre u
principali attività del S
degli avvenimenti vat
E aggiornato quotidia
Le immagini sono pr
Vaticano (CTV), i test
Vaticana (RV) e dal C
Le videonews offron
posizioni più autorev
principali questioni c
I link permettono lac
ufficiali dei documen

Country: **Holy See (Va**

Report p

Altri video sulla C
nel mondo

Connect with va

The Internet has changed more than individuals' daily lives. Social media sites, in particular, have redefined business and politics. By 2012, social media sites alone were selling more than $8 billion in ads. Total social media revenue in 2016 is expected to be $34 billion.[1] Beginning in 2008, social media also dominated political campaigns. Just before the 2008 presidential election, Barack Obama and his opponent, John McCain, together had close to 3 million Facebook supporters.[2] In 2009, the Obama administration announced on the White House blog that they had joined Twitter, Facebook, MySpace, YouTube, and Flickr. Their goal was "to create . . . unprecedented opportunity to connect you to

THE
VATICAN

ITALIANO ENGLISH ESPAÑOL DEUTSCH

Videos | Playlists

Subscribe

2008
urs ago

,642

a informativa delle
Benedetto XVI e
anti.

ntro Televisivo
dalla Radio

azione delle
sa cattolica sulle
ggi.
completi ed

te)

olation

0:00 / 1:14

Benedetto XVI. Appello per la pace in Medio Oriente.
From: vaticanit
Views: 421

Ultime notizie

Radio Vaticana
http://www.radiovaticana.org/it1/index.asp

Sala Stampa della Santa Sede
http://212.77.1.245/news_services/bulletin/bollettino.php...

ssage
annel

Political and religious figures and businesses are joining social media in order to reach more people.

your government in order to obtain information and services and to participate in policymaking."[3] Business and politics are going online.

The Rise of Online Shopping

In past generations, shopping required visiting a store, a brick-and-mortar building. Customers went to a store and bought an item, usually without shopping around. Now, many people find it more convenient to research and order products online. Consumers can either have products shipped directly to their doors or pick them up at a store. Online shoppers have access to more information online and can easily compare prices from different vendors. How did this change come about?

Online shopping began in the United Kingdom in 1979, when Michael Aldrich, an inventor and entrepreneur, used a telephone line to connect a television set to a computer. This led to the first business-to-business (B2B) shopping system. This connected the shopper directly to the seller's computer system, with no third-party involvement. B2B transactions in the 1980s involved holiday travel, vehicles, loan finance, and credit ratings. But television as a computer interface was limited, and communication lines needed much improvement. In the 1990s, business-to-consumer (B2C) online shopping became commercially viable with the upswing in use of PCs and the Internet. B2C was spurred by the launch of the World Wide Web in 1990. Charles Stack started the world's first online bookstore in 1992, Jeff Bezos

TIMELINE OF ONLINE SHOPPING SITES

SITE	LAUNCH YEAR	PURPOSE
Amazon.com	1995	Online bookseller
eBay	1995	Online auctions
Google.com	1998	Source of pre-purchase information
X.com (now PayPal)	1999	Way to pay online
AdWords (Google)	2000	Digital advertising
Apple iTunes	2003	Low-cost digital downloads
Groupon	2008	Group buying service with discount vouchers
Apple App Store	2008	Computer apps

Online shopping really began to take off with Amazon.com. The following list gives key sites relating to online shopping, and the dates they launched. In addition, most major brick-and-mortar stores, such as Wal-Mart, Sears, and Macy's, quickly added online sites.[5]

began Amazon.com in 1994, and eBay launched in 1996. Online shopping became much safer in 1994, when Netscape introduced a technology called SSL encryption, allowing secure transfer of online data.

Amazon.com founder and CEO Jeff Bezos is without doubt one of the most successful e-commerce entrepreneurs. In February 2015, his net worth was $32.5 billion.[4] In 1994, Bezos was a vice-president of a Wall Street firm when he began seeing the promise in online shopping. He looked at a number of products and settled on books for online sale

Jeff Bezos's Amazon.com continues to expand the e-commerce business.

because there was a large worldwide market and a huge selection of titles available, and books sold for a small price. He chose Seattle, Washington, to launch his new company because of its high-tech workforce and because there was a large book distribution center nearby in Oregon.

When Bezos launched Amazon.com in 1994, he focused on two aspects of the Internet: customers could browse and order directly from home, and sellers could collect almost limitless data on customers. Thus, the seller could determine each customer's likes and dislikes, allowing targeted marketing. Amazon.com began as an online bookseller. Twenty years later, more than one-half of independent booksellers in the United States were out of business, and Borders, one of two large chains, had declared bankruptcy. Steve Wasserman of *The Nation* magazine describes Amazon.com as a "steamroller," smashing all rivals.[6] And Bezos did not stop with books. Amazon.com now also sells music, movies, television shows, and many other products and services. Among other acquisitions, Bezos now owns the movie website IMDb.com and the shoe retailer Zappos.com.

Income from online shopping is growing rapidly at both web-based stores such as Amazon.com and at websites for traditional retail stores. B2C sales in the United States rose from $72 to $322 billion dollars between 2002 and 2013—an increase of almost 450 percent.[7] This trend is most evident in holiday shopping. During the 2013 holiday shopping season, store traffic was 50 percent less than it had been three years previously, whereas online spending increased by 10 percent.[8] The traditional beginning of the holiday shopping season is Black Friday, the first Friday after Thanksgiving. In 2005, the Monday after Thanksgiving became Cyber Monday, the traditional online shopping day. In 2013, Cyber Monday online shopping sales overtook Black Friday shopping in stores. Cyber Monday sales increased 20.6 percent over the previous year.[9]

Will online shopping mean the end of brick-and-mortar stores? University of Pennsylvania professor David Bell thinks not. He notes that the real world is still important, even as online sales increase. Online sales are more important in isolated markets because they offer consumers more choices. But seeing and touching the product in person can only happen at brick-and-mortar stores. Sometimes, shopping becomes a mixture of the two. A customer does research and pricing online, chooses the best deal, and makes the purchase at a brick-and-mortar store. Or, alternatively, he or she looks at the product in a store and buys it for less online. The Apple Store offers a positive brick-and-mortar experience. Its inviting in-store layout allows customers to try out products and use mobile technology, and it has friendly, helpful customer service representatives. Commerce analyst Brian Walker says Internet shopping is forcing brick-and-mortar stores to change. Some will close. Others might transform stores into fulfillment centers, which receive, process, and send orders. Still others will follow the Apple Store's example and improve the in-store shopping experience.

Dot-com Boom and Bust

In 1992 and 1993, major investors were not interested in the Internet. They were excited about the coming technology of interactive television, in which people would be able to choose endings of movies and camera angles for sports events. But these technologies did not develop, and investors—including television and cable companies, media groups, and even Microsoft—looked for another investment. They settled on the Internet. The number of Internet users began growing rapidly in 1995, triggering a burst of new Internet-based businesses, or dot-coms. This led to the "dot-com bubble," a period of stock market investment and speculation lasting from 1995 through 2001.

A few companies that had great ideas and started early, such as Amazon.com, enjoyed spectacular success after the dot-com bust.

Inexperienced investors speculated in dot-com companies that were valued far above the profits they could be expected to generate. A few people realized the dot-com boom could not last. In December 1996, Alan Greenspan, then chairman of the Federal Reserve, warned against "irrational exuberance."[10] Some dot-coms resorted to shady business practices; others outsourced their business to other countries. The result was loss of investments and unemployment among tech workers. In mid-2000, the bubble burst. Many young dot-coms failed. Established ones survived only by making huge layoffs.

Politics and the Internet

According to Chris Saad, chief strategy officer at Echo, Barack Obama in 2008 was the first political candidate to use social media successfully to win a presidential election. Saad says, "It was the first campaign where social media was pervasive and he understood it and leveraged it."[11] He compared 2008 with the 1960 election, when the first televised presidential debates helped John F. Kennedy gain the White House. Social media—like television debates and advertisements in the past—is a new campaign tool, and the candidate who learns to use it successfully will likely win. The main uses for social media in a campaign, according to Saad, are to create content that people share, which aids in fund-raising, and to keep track of where the candidate stands in the race.

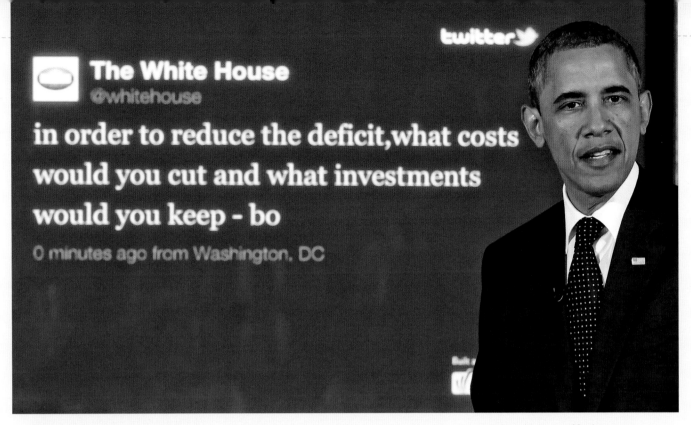

The White House
@whitehouse

in order to reduce the deficit, what costs would you cut and what investments would you keep - bo

0 minutes ago from Washington. DC

twitter

Obama had a successful social media campaign before the presidency and continued using social media in an effective way while in office.

During the 2008 campaign, 37 percent of voters between ages 18 and 24 obtained candidate information from social media such as Facebook.[12] Currently, most major political leaders, including heads of state, US cabinet members, and state governors are on Twitter. Even religious leaders, including the pope and the Dalai Lama, use Twitter.

SOCIAL MEDIA AND ACTIVISM

Does the use of social media generate activism that leads to social and political change? No, says Malcolm Gladwell in the *New Yorker*. Gladwell argues, "Facebook activism succeeds not by motivating people to make a real sacrifice but by motivating them to do the things that people do when they are not motivated enough to make a real sacrifice."[13] But Sarah Kessler on Mashable argues Internet-based social activism is in its infancy and has great potential. When Craig Kielburger founded Free the Children to fight childhood slavery, his Facebook page received approximately 174,000 hits in its first month. Approximately 20,000 people attended an event in Toronto for the cause, and 2,000 of them committed to a working trip overseas.[14]

Having a strong social media presence makes it easy for candidates to ask for and obtain political donations, and the Internet makes it much easier for small donors to contribute. With only a few clicks, they can send money, and their information is saved so they can contribute again later, with even fewer clicks—much simpler than writing a check. During campaign season, candidates and their promoters send a deluge of e-mails to individuals soliciting donations.

One downside to Internet political campaigning is its great capacity for quickly disseminating misinformation. Anne Mintz, author of *Web of Deception: Misinformation on the Internet*, says the spreading of misinformation about political candidates is not necessarily worse than in the past, but it is easier. But

Approximately 13 percent of adults donated to one of the presidential candidates during the 2012 elections. Of those who donated, 50 percent donated online or through e-mail, and 10 percent donated by text message.[15]

it is also easier to counter untrue claims. Mintz stresses that Internet readers must be informed consumers who use common sense and critical thinking when evaluating web information.

Widespread use of the Internet in business only began in the 1990s, and in politics, only in the 2000s. Thus, its effects are just beginning to be felt, and little research has so far been done to document changes it has caused. But as people continue experimenting with this powerful new tool, it is likely Internet influence—both positive and negative—will increase in the coming decades.

CHAPTER 8

THE
FUTURE

From its beginnings connecting a few military and university installations, the Internet has expanded into a vast, intricate, worldwide network. In 1993, the web opened information to everyone, and most have taken advantage of it. As of November 2014, 78.1 percent of US households had a high-speed Internet connection.[1] No one knows how the Internet will change in the future. But now, the system and its users are encountering several serious problems that need to be addressed.

Most US homes have computers or tablets with access to the Internet.

Social Networking Privacy

Privacy issues on social networking sites affect both teens and adults. The type of information shared can affect a person's privacy, safety, or reputation. According to a 2013 survey on the Pew Research Internet Study, teens are learning to manage their profiles. Many take steps to protect themselves, including keeping their profiles private or deleting people from their friends list. Teens' use of Twitter increased from 16 percent in 2011 to 24 percent in 2012.[2] According to danah boyd, author of *It's Complicated: The Social Lives of Networked Teens*, teens often see social media as their only opportunity to socialize freely with friends. Rules placed by authority figures, such as parents and teachers, limit their face-to-face time with friends. When these authority figures join Facebook, they are encroaching on the last bit of teens' freedom. In terms of privacy, boyd says teens worry less about strangers and more about authority figures. Parents, on the other hand, fear media sites lead their teens to share too much with strangers.

What teens share on a social networking site varies according to age, gender, and race. Boys ages 14 to 17 are more likely than girls to share cell phone numbers, and girls are more likely to be friends with teachers or coaches. In general, teens see their social networking accounts as extensions of their offline interactions. Most tweak their profile information to show themselves in their best light.

Adding to privacy and sharing concerns, Facebook and other sites watch all of their users. Major online companies monitor everyone's cyber footprints and use their likes and dislikes to match advertisements to users. A journalist for the *Atlantic* found that, when she opened the *New York Times* news site, NYTimes.com, she was tracked by 105 different companies whose sole purpose was to determine which ads should pop up when she went online.[3] The same thing happens on every site opened.

Companies also use online information in research to determine user preferences, health problems, and other information. Facebook, Twitter, Google, and Microsoft mine huge amounts of data from social communications. Facebook has used this data to study parent–child interactions, and Microsoft has used the data it collects to identify women having depression after childbirth. A Harvard-based study says, "Facebook is transformed from a public space to a behavioral laboratory."[4] That is, people who think they are using Facebook merely to communicate with friends are actually—inadvertently—supplying data not only to Facebook but to a variety of university researchers who are

TYPES OF MALWARE

Malware is malicious software that gets onto a computer and damages data or programs without the owner's knowledge or permission. Malware breaches the security of individual computers or networks and endangers people's privacy by stealing information. Computer owners today routinely install antiviral software, which protects against all types of malware. Some types of malware are named for the way they spread, such as a virus or worm. Other malware are named for their actions, such as spyware and adware.

using the data in their research projects, usually studying human behavior. Although the data collected does not specifically identify individuals, people are concerned about their privacy on these sites. Almost one-half of those who leave Facebook do so because of privacy concerns. They are right to be concerned, according to Ilka Gleibs, a social psychologist from the London School of Economics. Speaking of Facebook, she says, "Sometimes it's easier than we think to identify this data. . . . Be aware it is a space that is watched."[5]

Cyberattacks and Business Security

On November 24, 2014, unknown cybercriminals calling themselves Guardians of Peace hacked into the computers at Sony Pictures Entertainment. The thieves wanted to stop the release of the Seth Rogen and Evan Goldberg film *The Interview*, a satire involving the assassination of Kim Jong-un, the leader of North Korea. The attack temporarily paralyzed Sony's computer system and caused the release of a huge amount of sensitive and embarrassing information. This included private e-mails between Sony executives, unreleased scripts, illicit movie downloads, and personal information on Sony employees, from names and addresses to bank and credit card information, passwords, and more. Sony, fearing physical attacks on theaters, at first canceled release of *The Interview*, scheduled to open in theaters on Christmas Day. The company received considerable pressure for this decision. Most critics cited freedom of speech issues, stating that cancellation meant giving in to terrorists.

Sony eventually decided to release *The Interview*, but by that time, it was already available through video on demand.

On December 19, the Federal Bureau of Investigation (FBI) announced North Korea was definitely behind the attack, although North Korea continued denying involvement. The US government responded with sanctions, or penalties, against North Korea, but the damage to Sony and its employees had already been done. According to

Director of National Intelligence James Clapper, the North Korean attack on Sony was the "most serious" cyberattack ever made against US interests.

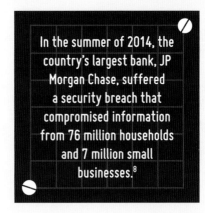

In the summer of 2014, the country's largest bank, JP Morgan Chase, suffered a security breach that compromised information from 76 million households and 7 million small businesses.[8]

Cyberattacks are not always politically motivated. During the 2013 holiday season, a major cyberbreach occurred at Target stores. Between Thanksgiving and Christmas, hackers stole credit and debit card information from more than 40 million shoppers, causing an upsurge in fraudulent credit card transactions.[6] Other large stores, including J. C. Penney, Wal-Mart, Best Buy, and Home Depot, have all been hacked in the last several years, but all say customer data were not stolen. Companies have improved their ability to detect invaders on their systems, but criminals have also developed more sophisticated attack schemes.

It is not easy to predict or overcome a cyberbreach. A study by McKinsey and Company finds 80 percent of CEOs worldwide say their organizations cannot adapt quickly enough to overcome increasingly sophisticated cyberattacks. The study predicts that by 2020, attacks could cause worldwide losses as great as $3 trillion in productivity and growth, and it stresses the need for new security methods.[7] Attackers include criminals, nation-states, and political "hactivists." Many attacks are aimed at governments, military installations, businesses, and banks. In a survey by the

Pew Research Internet Study, 61 percent of Internet experts believed that, before 2025, a major cyberattack would cause "widespread harm to a nation's security and capacity to defend itself and its people."[9] According to Jay Cross, chief scientist at Internet Time Group, "Connectedness begets vulnerability."[10]

Net Neutrality

Most of the power determining the speed of Internet service, particularly streaming of media such as movies, is currently in the hands of Internet service providers (ISPs). The largest ISPs, such as Comcast and Verizon, have the greatest power. They can choose to give preferential treatment to giant websites such as Amazon.com and Netflix—that is, they can transfer data from these sites to consumers rapidly, while slowing down transfer of data from, say, Joe Smith's tiny personal website. As demand for streaming media rises, many consumers are becoming more worried about the power in the hands of these giants. They think ISPs should be regulated to ensure net neutrality, or equal treatment for all content on the Internet.

If net neutrality is practiced, all broadband network providers should send all information through the Internet at equal speeds and quality, without regard to its source. As tech writer Andrew Lumby explains, "Net neutrality is, at its core, the concept that every piece of information on the public Internet should be as accessible as any other. . . . Access to this information should not be in any way stifled by your Internet service provider (ISP)."[11] Net neutrality means a free

Lack of net neutrality would affect how consumers obtain information and entertainment—and how much they pay for it.

and open Internet, or a level playing field for all companies. Most people, if they must wait too long for a site to load, get frustrated and go to another site. Without net neutrality, its advocates fear that large companies will stifle start-ups by slowing access to their sites and steering Internet traffic only to their own sites.

The innovators who started the Internet using collaborative peer networks are fiercely committed to maintaining net neutrality. Web founder Tim Berners-Lee is one of the most outspoken. But, according to Robert McMillan, writing for *Wired*, net neutrality does not exist. Instead, huge companies such as Google, Facebook, and Netflix have direct connections to large ISPs such as Comcast and Verizon, which act as Internet "fast lanes." The FCC regulates telephone services, but has not traditionally regulated ISPs. In February 2015 the FCC announced a new policy to treat ISPs as "public utilities" that can be regulated in the public interest, and used this new power to mandate net neutrality. Opponents have already raised strenuous objections.

The Internet and the Future

How else is the Internet likely to change? First, data speeds will likely become much faster. The present record for data transmission speed is 100 petabits per second, or 100 billion megabits per second—equivalent to downloading 400 DVDs worth of data per second.[12] As the cost of ultrahigh speed transmission decreases, every consumer should be able to download movies or play videos with no lag time.

Between now and 2025, 83 percent of computer experts foresee an expansion in the Internet of Things, including embedded and wearable devices.[13] Most think this expansion will be beneficial. The Internet of Things refers to the networking of objects such as home appliances and cars as well as devices on and in the body. Examples include under-skin sensors that monitor a patient's vital signs, remote control apps that allow individuals to control household activities from their cell phones, and "smart cities" with apps to control traffic flow. A few people either think these

types of applications will not become widespread, or will not be beneficial. Some see them as toys for the very rich. Others fear they will destroy the last remnants of privacy. Law professor Frank Pasquale of the University of Maryland says the Internet of Things in the workplace will become "like an 'ankle monitor' of the mind that upgrades scanning not merely to location, but also to observable 'outputs' like typing and eye movements."[14] That is, people on the Internet will be able to monitor not only where a person is, but also his or her medical signs and even personal movements. Pasquale sees people in the future being divided into a small group of "watchers" and a much larger group of those watched, manipulated, and experimented on.

There will likely be many unforeseen changes in the coming decades, and these changes will affect society. What is certain is that the Internet's exceedingly rapid rate of change shows no signs of slowing. This means the shape of the future will certainly be different, even if experts cannot predict exactly how.

Wearable technology such as the Apple Watch could be the future of the Internet.

THE NEXT
GENERATION: INTERNET OF THINGS

tems around us— electronic heart monitors, microchips in farm animals, or GPS tracking collars on pets—have slowly become smart; that is, they can receive, process, and send information. In the future, the human body, home, city, industry, and environment will all contain embedded sensors that interact with people through smartphones or other Internet links. These sensors will enhance human senses and provide people with continuous, detailed information about their surroundings.

Smartphones already contain apps to monitor an individual's daily activities, such as location and workout details. Room or body sensors can monitor a baby or an elderly person's activities, or a person's heartbeat or respiration, and send this information to a caregiver or

Home automation system

Smart grid

doctor. In the home, sensors will monitor heating, appliances, lights, and motion, and they will send the information directly to the individual's smartphone. In the smart city, sensors will monitor streetlights, electricity use, and availability of parking spaces. Smart grids in the electrical power industry will automate and optimize the flow of electricity, saving energy and money. In industry, embedded sensors will monitor equipment, worker safety, and manufacturing quality. In the environment, sensors will monitor everything from air and water pollution to wildlife movements to illegal deforestation. As the Internet of Things expands, technologies that today are still novelties, such as drones and driverless cars, will become an ordinary part of the future.

Baby monitor

Camera Drone

DATE OF INVENTION

October 29, 1969: the first two nodes on the Internet are connected and send the first message

KEY PLAYERS

▶ Leonard Kleinrock, connected the first two nodes on the Internet

▶ Ray Tomlinson and Lawrence Roberts, developers of e-mail program

▶ Robert Kahn and Vint Cerf, creators of the TCP/IP protocol

▶ Tim Berners-Lee, creator of the World Wide Web

KEY TECHNOLOGIES

The development of web programs, including HTTP, HTML, and browsers, made the World Wide Web possible. Digital computer messages are transformed into light, which travels through fiber-optic cables. At their destination, signals are first transformed back into digital form and then into understandable forms. Different browsers make it possible for computers with different operating systems to access the web. Cloud computing greatly increases individuals' access to data and makes collaboration easier. Wi-Fi technology makes it much easier to access the Internet from any location. The cell phone and smartphone make Internet technology "wearable" and thus enable users to access the Internet while moving from place to place.

EVOLUTION AND UPGRADES

▶ ARPANET, 1973

▶ NSFNET, 1986

▶ Domain name system (DNS), 1983

▶ World Wide Web (WWW), 1991

IMPACT ON SOCIETY

ARPANET improved communications among military and university scientists. Opening of the web to everyone made it easy to use and enabled people to find information, and upload their own information by developing personal or business-related websites. Development of search engines, particularly Google, allowed people to retrieve information instantaneously. Cloud computing allowed individuals to store their data outside their own computers and retrieve it from anywhere. The smartphone made it possible to communicate "on the go," and changed public spaces, making them more personal but less private. Social networking and social media brought a sharp increase in person-to-person communication and in the sharing of personal ideas and information through blogs, videos, and photos. It increased the visibility of many social issues. The rapid growth of online shopping increased beginning in 2005, and businesses and entrepreneurs have steadily increased their reliance on the web to advertise and build their customer bases. Security and privacy are major issues on the Internet, particularly with regard to social media and social networking.

QUOTE

"Cyberspace comes out from behind the screen . . . and moves out into your physical space so that there will be intelligence and embedded technology in the walls of your room, in your desk, in your fingernails."

—*Leonard Kleinrock*

algorithm

A set of rules followed in mathematical computations and computer problem solving.

application

A computer program, or piece of software, designed to enable the user to carry out a function.

domain name system (DNS)

An automatic system for naming locations on the Internet.

fiber-optic cable

A bundle of extremely thin strands of glass that carries digital information long distances.

file sharing

The process of transmitting and sharing files between computers using a network such as the Internet.

hypertext markup language (HTML)

The Internet language protocol used to transmit information over the web.

local area network

An independently managed network in a localized area, such as a company, having many connected, resource-sharing workstations with individual users.

malware

Any type of malicious or deliberately harmful software, including viruses, worms, spyware, adware, and bots.

microfilm

Film carrying small photographic records of printed pages of things such as newspapers or magazines.

modem

A device that connects one computer to another and transfers data over telephone lines.

net neutrality

The principle that all broadband network providers should send all information through the Internet at equal speeds and quality, without regard to its source.

node

A central or connecting point where lines or pathways intersect or branch.

open access

All documents and programs relating to Internet development on the Internet that are free and accessible to everyone.

packet switching

The process that breaks down large amounts of data into small chunks (packets) that can move unhindered through a network and be reassembled at the other end.

Request for Comments (RFC)

Means of sharing information about Internet research; developed into specification documents and later protocols for new Internet procedures.

router

A device that forwards data packets along networks; must be connected to at least two networks and is located at a gateway, the place where the networks connect.

server

A computer that manages files and shares them with other computers.

SELECTED BIBLIOGRAPHY

Blum, Andrew. *Tubes: A Journey to the Center of the Internet*. New York: Ecco, 2012. Print.

Burkeman, Oliver. "Forty Years of the Internet: How the World Changed Forever." *Guardian*. Guardian News and Media Limited, Oct. 22, 2009. Web. Oct. 5, 2014.

Johnson, Steven. "The Internet? We Built That." *New York Times Magazine*. New York Times, Sept. 21, 2012. Web. Oct. 12, 2014.

Ryan, Johnny. *A History of the Internet and the Digital Future*. London, UK: Reaktion, 2010. Print.

FURTHER READINGS

Lusted, Marcia Amidon. *Social Networking: MySpace, Facebook, & Twitter*. Minneapolis: Abdo, 2011. Print.

Rowell, Rebecca. *YouTube: The Company and Its Founders*. Minneapolis: Abdo, 2011. Print.

Szumski, Bonnie. *How Are Online Activities Affecting Society?* San Diego: ReferencePoint, 2013. Print.

WEBSITES

To learn more about Essential Library of Inventions, visit **booklinks.abdopublishing.com**. These links are routinely monitored and updated to provide the most current information available.

FOR MORE INFORMATION

For more information on this subject, contact or visit the following organizations:

International Telecommunication Union

Place des Nations
1211 Geneva 20 Switzerland
+41-22-730-5111
http://www.itu.int/en/Pages/default.aspx

This international organization is dedicated to ensuring fair play regarding Internet use around the world. It is responsible for assigning radio frequencies on Earth and in space.

Internet Engineering Task Force

48377 Fremont Boulevard, Suite 117
Fremont, CA 94538
510-492-4080
https://www.ietf.org/

The IETF is an organized activity of the Internet Society. Its purpose is to make the Internet work better by producing high quality technical documents such as RFCs that teach people how to better design, manage, and use the Internet.

Internet Society

1775 Wiehle Avenue, Suite 201
Reston, VA 20190
703-439-2120
http://www.internetsociety.org

The Internet Society is an organization dedicated to promoting "the open development, evolution, and use of the internet for the benefit of all people throughout the world." The website describes their work and includes up-to-date news about the Internet and short articles on how the Internet works.

SOURCE NOTES

Chapter 1. The Internet Is Born

1. Oliver Burkeman. "Forty Years of the Internet: How the World Changed Forever." *Guardian*. Guardian News and Media Limited, 23 Oct. 2009. Web. 5 Oct. 2014.

2. Ibid.

3. Philip Rosenbaum. "Web Pioneer Recalls 'Birth of the Internet.'" *The University of California*. Leonard Kleinrock, 18 Jan. 2010. Web. 11 Mar. 2015.

4. Vangie Beal. "Internet." *Webopedia*. QuinStreet Inc., 2015. Web. 15 Nov. 2014.

5. Andrew Blum. *Tubes: A Journey to the Center of the Internet*. New York: Ecco, 2012. Print. 4.

6. "Internet Usage Statistics: The Internet Big Picture." *Internet World Stats*. Miniwatts Marketing Group, 3 Feb. 2015. Web. 11 Mar. 2015.

7. Andrew Blum. *Tubes: A Journey to the Center of the Internet*. New York: Ecco, 2012. Print. 7–8.

8. Ibid. 192–194.

Chapter 2. Creating the Internet

1. Oliver Burkeman. "Forty Years of the Internet: How the World Changed Forever." *Guardian*. Guardian News and Media Limited, 23 Oct. 2009. Web. 5 Oct. 2014.

2. James Pelkey. "Chapter 2: Networking: Vision and Packet Switching 1959–1968. Intergalactic Vision to Arpanet." *Entrepreneurial Capitalism and Innovation: A History of Computer Communications 1968–1988*. James Pelkey, 2007. Web. 1 Nov. 2014.

3. William Stewart. "ARPANET—The First Internet." *The Living Internet*. William Stewart, 2014. Web. 11 Mar. 2015.

Chapter 3. Internet for Everyone

1. Steven Johnson. "The Internet? We Built That." *New York Times Magazine*. New York Times Company, 21 Sept. 2012. Web. 12 Oct. 2014.

2. Oliver Burkeman. "Forty Years of the Internet: How the World Changed Forever." *Guardian*. Guardian News and Media Limited, 23 Oct. 2009. Web. 5 Oct. 2014.

3. Ibid.

4. KeriLynn Engel. "Is the Internet Running Out of Room?" *Who Is Hosting This?* WhoIsHostingThis.com, 2014. Web. 11 Mar. 2015.

5. Marshall Brain and Stephanie Crawford. "How Domain Name Servers Work." *How Stuff Works*. How Stuff Works, 1 Apr. 2000. Web. 5 Jan. 2015.

6. Barry M. Leiner, et al. "Brief History of the Internet." *Internet Society*. Internet Society, 15 Oct. 2012. Web. 1 Oct. 2014.

7. "10 Descriptions of Offerings from Early ISP's." *Internet Service*. Internet Service, 2015. Web. 4 Nov. 2014.

8. "Want Pain? Try Loading Today's Websites over Dial-up." *Pingdom*. Pingdom AB, 15 June 2012. Web. 12 Jan. 2015.

Chapter 4. Changing the World

1. Lenny Zeltser. "Early History of the World-Wide Web: Origins and Beyond." *Lenny Zeltser*. Lenny Zeltser, 8 Feb. 2015. Web. 11 Mar. 2015.

2. James Vincent. "The Web Is 25: 10 Things You Need to Know about the Web (Including How Much It Weighs)." *Independent*. independent.co.uk, 12 Mar. 2014. Web. 9 Oct. 2014.

3. Jonathan Owen. "25 Years of the World Wide Web: Tim Berners-Lee Explains How It All Began." *Independent*. independent.co.uk, 12 Mar. 2014. Web. 9 Oct. 2014.

4. Johnny Ryan. *A History of the Internet and the Digital Future*. London: Reaktion, 2010. Print. 115–116.

Chapter 5. Search Engines

1. "Larry Page and Sergey Brin." *Entrepreneur*. Entrepreneur, 15 Oct. 2008. Web. 7 Nov. 2014.

2. Ibid.

3. "Our History in Depth." *Google*. Google, 2015. Web. 11 Mar. 2015.

4. Ibid.

5. "Google Inc. Announces Fourth Quarter and Fiscal Year 2013 Results." *Google*. Google, 30 Jan. 2014. Web. 7 Nov. 2014.

6. Mahafreed Irani. "Google Turns 15: How It Has Changed Our Lives." *DNA*. Diligent Media Corporation, 5 Sept. 2013. Web. 6 Nov. 2014.

7. Jennifer Woodard Maderazo. "How Google, Wikipedia Have Changed Our Lives—For Better and Worse." *PBS*. Public Broadcasting Service, 25 Jan. 2008. Web. 6 Nov. 2014.

8. Mahafreed Irani. "Google Turns 15: How It Has Changed Our Lives." *DNA*. Diligent Media Corporation, 5 Sept. 2013. Web. 6 Nov. 2014.

9. Daven Hiskey. "Where the Word 'Wiki' Comes From." *Today I Found Out*. Vacca Foeda Media, 2012. Web. 9 Nov. 2014.

10. "*Wikipedia* of Jimmy Wales and Larry Sanger." *History of Computers*. Georgi Dalakov, 6 Nov. 2014. Web. 9. 2014.

11. Roy Rosenweig. "Can History Be Open Source? Wikipedia and the Future of the Past." *Roy Rosenweig Center for History and New Media*. Roy Rosenweig Center for History and New Media, 2015. Web. 9 Nov. 2014.

12. Jennifer Woodard Maderazo. "How Google, Wikipedia Have Changed Our Lives—For Better and Worse." *PBS*. Public Broadcasting Service, 25 Jan. 2008. Web. 6 Nov. 2014.

13. "10 Ways Wikipedia Has Changed Education." *Online Courses*. Online College Courses, 21 June 2011. Web. 9 Nov. 2014.

Chapter 6. Social Sites

1. Scott W. Campbell and Yong Jin Park. "Social Implications of Mobile Telephony: The Rise of Personal Communication Society." *Sociology Compass*. Blackwell Publishing, 2008. Web. 4 Nov. 2014.

2. Stephanie Buck. "Cell-ebration! 40 Years of Cellphone History." *Mashable*. Mashable, 3 Apr. 2013. Web. 9 Jan. 2015.

3. Ibid.

4. Ibid.

5. Scott W. Campbell and Yong Jin Park. "Social Implications of Mobile Telephony: The Rise of Personal Communication Society." *Sociology Compass*. Blackwell, 2008. Web. 4 Nov. 2014.

6. Ibid.

7. Ibid.

8. "The Brief History of Social Media." *University of North Carolina at Pembroke*. The University of North Carolina at Pembroke, 2014. Web. 10 Jan. 2015.

9. Ibid.

10. "Top 15 Most Popular Social Networking Sites | March 2015." *eBiz*. eBizMBA, 2015. Web. 11 Mar. 2015.

11. Seth Masket. "Don't Fear the Network: The Internet Is Changing the Way We Communicate for the Better." *Pacific Standard*. The Miller-McCune Center for Research, Media and Public Policy, 2 June 2014. Web. 4 Nov. 2014.

Chapter 7. Business and Politics

1. "Social Networking: Pros and Cons." *ProCon.org*. ProCon.org, 23 Sept. 2014. Web. 11 Nov. 2014.

2. Ibid.

3. Ibid.

4. "The World's Billionaires." *Forbes*. Forbes.com, 2 Mar. 2015. Web. 11 Mar. 2015.

5. Dr. Fiona Ellis-Chadwick. "History of Online Retail." *The Open University*. The Open University, 14 Oct. 2013. Web. 11 Jan. 2015.

6. Steve Wasserman. "The Amazon Effect." *The Nation*. The Nation, 29 May 2012. Web. 13 Nov. 2014.

7. "Annual B2C e-commerce Sales in the United States from 2002 to 2013 (In Billion U.S. Dollars)." *The Statistics Portal*. Statista, 2013. Web. 11 Mar. 2015.

8. Brian K Walker. "Retail in Crisis: These Are the Changes Brick-and-Mortar Stores Must Make." *Forbes*. Forbes.com, 12 Feb. 2014. Web. 12 Nov. 2014.

9. Morgan Korn. "Cyber Monday Trumps Black Friday: Why Online Shopping is Winning." *Yahoo! Finance*. Yahoo!, 3 Dec. 2013. Web. 12 Nov. 2014.

10. Johnny Ryan. *A History of the Internet and the Digital Future*. London: Reaktion, 2010. Print. 124.

11. Laura Jerpi. "Political Campaigns and Social Media—Tweeting Their Way Into Office." *South Source*. South University, Oct. 2012. Web. 13 Nov. 2014.

12. "Social Networking: Pros and Cons." *ProCon. org*. ProCon.org, 23 Sept. 2014. Web. 11 Nov. 2014.

13. Malcolm Gladwell. "Small Change: Why the Revolution Will Not Be Tweeted." *New Yorker*. Conde Nast, 4 Oct. 2010. Web 13 Nov. 2014.

14. Sarah Kessler. "Why Social Media Is Reinventing Activism." *Mashable*. Mashable.com, 9 Oct. 2010. Web. 13 Nov. 2014.

15. Aaron Smith and Maeve Duggan. "Presidential Campaign Donations in the Digital Age." *Pew Research Center*. Pew Research Center, 25 Oct. 2012. Web. 13 Nov. 2014.

Chapter 8. The Future

1. "Nearly 8 in 10 Americans Have Access to High-Speed Internet." *United States Census Bureau*. US Department of Commerce, 13 Nov. 2014. Web. 16 Nov. 2014.

2. Mary Madden, et al. "Teens, Social Media, and Privacy." *Pew Research Center*. Pew Research Center, 21 May 2013. Web. 16 Nov. 2014.

3. Alexis C. Madrigal. "I'm Being Followed: How Google—and 104 Other Companies—Are Tracking Me on the Web." *Atlantic*. Atlantic Monthly Group, 29 Feb. 2012. Web. 12 Jan. 2015.

4. Sharon Jayson. "Social Media Research Raises Privacy and Ethics Issues." *USA Today*. USA Today, 12 Mar. 2014. Web. 16 Nov. 2014.

5. Ibid.

6. Jim Finkle and Dhanya Skariachan. "Target Cyber Breach Hits 40 Million Payment Cards at Holiday Peak." *Reuters*. Thomson Reuters, 19 Dec. 2013. Web. 15 Nov. 2014.

7. Brian Taylor. "Cyberattacks Fallout Could Cost the Global Economy $3 Trillion By 2020." *TechRepublic*. CBS Interactive, 20 Feb. 2014. Web. 15 Nov. 2014.

8. Danielle Douglas-Gabriel. "JPMorgan Says 76 Million Households Were Affected by Cyber Breach." *Washington Post*. Washington Post, 2 Oct. 2014. Web. 18 Nov. 2014.

9. Lee Rainie, Janna Anderson, and Jennifer Connolly. "Cyber Attacks Likely to Increase." *Pew Research Center*. Pew Research Center, 29 Oct. 2014. Web. 17 Nov. 2014.

10. Ibid.

11. Andrew Lumby. "The Net Neutrality Debate Explained." *CNBC*. CNBC, 17 Nov. 2014. Web. 17 Nov. 2014.

12. Jonathan Strickland. "What Is the Future of the Internet?" *HowStuffWorks*. HowStuffWorks, 10 May 2010. Web. 17 Nov. 2014.

13. Janna Anderson and Lee Rainie. "The Internet of Things Will Thrive by 2025." *Pew Research Center*. Pew Research Center, 14 May 2014. Web. 18 Nov. 2014.

14. Ibid.

INDEX

About the Author

Carol Hand has a PhD in zoology with a specialization in marine ecology. She has taught college, worked for standardized testing companies, developed multimedia science and technology curricula, and written more than 20 science and technology books for young people. She has used the Internet extensively, and she can no longer imagine life without Google!